CW00544364

Cracking Creative Writing

100+ Activities to Improve KS2 Children's Writing Confidence

David Horner

Dedication

For Judith

We hope you and your pupils enjoy using the ideas in this book. Brilliant Publications publishes many other books to help primary school teachers. To find out more details on all of our titles, including those listed below, please go to our website: www.brilliantpublications.co.uk.

Brilliant Activities for Creative Writing Series

Year 1   978-0-85747-463-6
Year 2   978-0-85747-464-3
Year 3   978-0-85747-465-0
Year 4   978-0-85747-466-7
Year 5   978-0-85747-467-4
Year 6   978-0-85747-468-1

Boost Creative Writing Series

5-7 Year Olds   978-1-78317-058-6
7-9 Year Olds   978-1-78317-059-3
9-11 Year Olds 978-1-78317-060-9

Getting to Grips with English Grammar

Year 1   978-1-78317-215-3
Year 2   978-1-78317-216-0
Year 3   978-1-78317-217-7
Year 4   978-1-78317-218-4
Year 5   978-1-78317-219-1
Year 6   978-1-78317-220-7

Published by Brilliant Publications Limited
Unit 10
Sparrow Hall Farm
Edlesborough
Dunstable
Bedfordshire
LU6 2ES, UK

Email: info@brilliantpublications.co.uk
Website: www.brilliantpublications.co.uk
Tel: 01525 222292

The name Brilliant Publications and the logo are registered trademarks.

Written by David Horner
Illustrated by Gaynor Berry
Front cover illustration by Brilliant Publications Limited

© Brilliant Publications Limited 2019
Printed ISBN   978-0-85747-831-3
e-pdf ISBN   978-0-85747-832-0

First printed and published in the UK in 2020

The right of David Horner to be identified as the author of this work has been asserted by himself in accordance with the Copyright, Designs and Patents Act 1988.

Pages 7–111 may be photocopied by individual teachers acting on behalf of the purchasing institution for classroom use only, without permission from the publisher or declaration to the Copyright Licensing Agency or the Publishers' Licensing Services. The materials may not be reproduced in any other form or for any other purpose without the prior permission of the publisher.

Contents

Introduction

'Writing is the greatest human invention.' – Professor Brian Cox

Writing matters. It matters to us as teachers, and it certainly matters to children - they want to be able to do it, and be good at it. As teachers, we want children to write successfully and also enjoy the activity itself. Perhaps even find it fun.

However, children will only do so if they feel their writing will be productive and successful, and not be a path to failure and criticism. Every written task we set children teaches them something - good or bad - about writing and their relationship to it. Thus, our key task is to give them as many activities with as high a chance of success as we possibly can. This collection of ideas is my small contribution to that quest.

The standing joke with my kids was that it didn't really matter what dad got up to – mum had a proper job. My wife worked in IT, while my 'improper' job had me going here, there and anywhere, running creative writing workshops for youngsters. My wife gave up the IT career for work in the charitable sector, while I just kept on going - and going - over hundreds and hundreds of school visits. This book is the product of those days and the writing activities I came up with. I always offered to run a fresh activity for each different class or group of children through the day. Often, I was lucky enough to be invited back to places and this meant each time creating a whole new round of activities. I did like that challenge – and hence the more than one hundred items here. Of course, I would always plan my day's work, but there were times when a teacher would ask once I'd arrived if I had an idea on a particular issue; or sometimes an issue would suddenly emerge from a casual staffroom chat. Many of the ideas featuring grammatical points, surface features and literary terms came about that way: because, if I could come up with something, those elements would be embedded and reinforced within the creative idea. And, of course, I know these ideas work – they've been classroom tested, some of them many, many times over!

I regularly found that, given a clear, structured approach, children could engage with, even relish the pace of creating a piece of work in (sometimes well under) an hour. They would discover that writing didn't have to be slow and unproductive; by engaging in the activity, they were inevitably developing their concentration and writing stamina - growing in confidence in their abilities and starting to see themselves as real writers writing for real.

Each idea in this collection adopts the same format: I've written each one directly to the writers, taking a recipe-style, step-by-step approach and offering a worked example at the very start, so individuals can see the kind of outcome they are aiming for. Alternatively, a teacher can choose to use any of the ideas to teach as a group or whole class activity. As you will see, most of the examples of children's writing come from them working individually, in pairs or in small, collaborative groups. This was deliberate on my part as I really did want young writers to experience a feeling of success that was very much their own. However, there are also pieces here produced by class-size, and larger, groups. These were created, usually with me scribing, say, for a very mixed age gathering at a holiday playscheme, or as a starter activity with a large group specially put together for the occasion: an able pupil day, a day for children from different small schools heading for the same high school, for example.

The ideas here cover a great range of writing-related features and terms as well as some creative routes into those trickier aspects of English grammar and punctuation I mentioned earlier. Some are straightforward, others more demanding. Rather than using decontextualized exercises, these activities invite young writers to explore the language. The children's own creative writing becomes the context for their playing with, and thus learning about, the language – how it works, its rules, its possibilities – and crucially therefore, what they can do with it. These are not 'free' writing activities; each has its specific challenges, constraints and formal game plan. If a child could benefit from using, say, a dictionary or thesaurus for a particular idea, then they are told this at the outset.

Time, as every teacher knows, is the elephant in the room, and so there were times when writing had to be a one-shot affair – and that could be perfectly fine: 'Just see what you have produced in 20 minutes!' With more time available, the session could allow for initial research, planning, note-making, drafting – in short, the real and regular activities of all real writers. My simple objective was for children to have a period of genuine enjoyment with the process of writing and feel pleasure and satisfaction with the final written product.

More than twenty years ago, that great teacher Jill Pirrie wrote, 'There is no more intimidating threshold than the blank piece of paper.' That sentence has haunted me – and challenged me to devise ways of helping young writers cross that threshold – regularly, confidently, ambitiously. For above all, children need to feel in control of English and not be oppressed by a belief that it controls them.

To finish, a big thankyou to all the headteachers, class teachers, librarians, play scheme leaders who lent me those young writers - and thanks to them too. It really was a lot of cracking creative fun.

What If an Elephant Married a Fridge?

You'd get an elephridge!

The elephridge is white as snow and grey as concrete.
It has a large door in its front and also a long, bendy trunk.
Its skin is as hot as the sun, but inside it is freezing cold.
Its sound is a soft rumble and a loud trumpeting.
It looks after your food, and will only eat electricity and grass.
It can stand completely still in your house and walk forever across Africa.

Eleanor

Now it's your turn.

First, read all the details below before you start your writing.

✳   If such a thing as an elephridge (or a fridgiphant) could exist, it would be what we call a hybrid. A hybrid animal is the offspring of two different species. So, a mule is a hybrid, born from a horse and a donkey. Some modern cars are hybrids; they have both a petrol and an electric engine.

✳   You are now going to create your own hybrid. A most unusual one.

✳   Begin by choosing one animal. It can be a wild one, or a farm one, or a pet one. An extinct one. One that flies, one that swims, one that lives on land. You choose.

✳   Note down some brief details of your chosen animal: where it lives; its size and shape; its colouring; any sounds it makes; what it does; what it eats.

✳   Now choose a machine. It can be large or small. It can be bang up to date or very old fashioned. It can be a machine found in the home, or on the roads, or on a building site, or…. It might run on petrol, coal, nuclear power, rocket fuel. You choose.

✳   Note down some details of your chosen machine: its size and appearance; where you normally find it; its noise; what fuel it uses; what it does.

✳   Now start putting both your lists together to make your hybrid. Put every pair of details onto a new line. The more items you include, the more your hybrid comes to life.

✳   Finally, see if the two names of your chosen machine and animal can be mashed together to make one exciting new name.

Come Indoors, Outdoors!

*It looked so cold and
miserable outside, I
opened the window and shouted to it to
come in. In it rushed, the winter wind, with a huge
and horrible howl. It whirled round my room
like a massive cloak. I thought I was trapped inside a
tumble drier.
My bed got thrown upside down. My books
flew round my head like mad birds.
Finally,
the wind sat down on my carpet.
I said,
"I think you'd better leave now."*

Johanna

Think back to Raymond Briggs' classic 1978 picture book *The Snowman*. It starts, you'll recall, when the boy builds his snowman. Then, in the middle of the night, he invites the snowman inside. And that is where the adventures begin.

What if we now take things a bit further and invite the actual weather indoors? Not all of it, but just one element? For example:

sunshine   frost   a thunderstorm   a rainbow   snow   an April shower   fog   a breeze

Choose one of these, or an idea of your own. And choose a room to invite the weather into.

✳ This is going to be a piece of free verse, or open form, with no fixed rhyme scheme or set rhythm. Instead, you are going to write as if you are speaking. You'll be writing out loud.

✳ First, sit and focus on the room and yourself in it. Imagine the scene unfolding as you ask your weather inside and what happens when you do. See it all as a cartoon, if it helps. Let your thoughts run as wild as your weather! Jot down details that come to you – just single words.

✳ These jottings are your key words and you can now build your poem around them. Feel free to include alliteration, simile, metaphor as you write. These all add to the drama.

✳ You might prefer to write a first draft in prose. Read what you've written out loud to yourself and mark the line breaks wherever you naturally make pauses.

✳ Now write a final draft, with the line breaks as you marked them. It's entirely up to you to decide just where and how you will finish the adventure.

How to Look Different

How to Look Different

My hat will be a black thunder cloud.
I shall wear a coat woven from sixty April showers
and a dress made from Japanese fog.

I'll make my scarf from a single rainbow.
My gloves will be fashioned from Spanish sunbeams
and both my shoes will be bolts of lightning.

Ayesha

Well, Ayesha would certainly look different in clothes made from the weather!

And now it's your turn. Be sure you read all the details below before you start writing.

✳ Write down at least six items of clothing you like wearing.

✳ Choose a theme for your 'different' look. You can have the weather again, or:

> *foods   flowers   outer space   sea life   plastic   sweet things   a season*

✳ Or, you might think of a theme of your own.

✳ Beside each of your items of clothing write an item from your chosen theme.

✳ Now write your description – one line for each item of clothing. Look back at Ayesha's piece to see how she added details to each bit of weather to bring it to life.

✳ See also how she began the lines of her writing in different ways.

****

✳ **Note:** This writing idea comes from the paintings of Giuseppe Arcimboldo. He is famous for painting heads – made out of all sorts of everyday things, such as books, fishes and birds. He lived in Milan, Italy, nearly 500 years ago.

Russian Dolls

Russian Dolls

I hid a cup in Huddersfield and put the cold, dark church inside.

I placed a jar in Tennessee and kept ten lightning bolts in it.

I left a cornflakes box in Japan. My sister's platform shoes are in there.

I dropped a bucket in the North Sea filled with bullies.

I buried a barrel in the Sahara Desert with all the Action Men I used to love.

Nathan

You'll know what Russian dolls are: one large wooden doll, made of two halves and when you split the halves, you find another smaller doll hidden inside, with another even smaller doll hidden inside, and so on. Usually you get five dolls all together.

Those dolls are the idea behind this writing activity, which is all about hiding things. And as well as hiding things in your poem, you are also going to craftily hide a line. The line is, 'I placed a jar in Tennessee', from the poem 'Anecdote of the Jar' by the American poet Wallace Stevens. You'll see it there in Nathan's poem.

Now it's your turn. Be sure you read all the details below before you start writing. Have a thesaurus handy.

✳ It's choosing time. Write each of your choices in note form:

✳ First, choose five containers – one of which must be a jar. Write them down in the order of their size. You can go from smallest to largest – for example, egg cup to trunk – or largest to smallest – for example, suitcase to thimble. You decide and use your thesaurus if it helps.

✳ Next, choose five things to hide in each container. These can be your favourite things, things you dislike, favourite things of people you know, impossible things, things you've left behind. You decide.

✳ Now choose five different 'putting' verbs, one of which must be 'placed'. Look back at Nathan's choices and aim to use four different ones to him. Use your thesaurus if it helps.

✳ Finally, choose five hiding places – one of which must be Tennessee. These can be any places you like – more American states, places in your home area, cities from round the world, places all beginning with 'T'. You decide.

✳ You're ready now to turn those notes into the five lines of your poem. You can use Nathan's lines as your model. Of course, one of the lines will be the hidden Tennessee line! Don't forget to write the title at the top.

✳ Finally, and only if you like the idea, you can tell your readers about that hidden line by writing, 'A poem including a line by Wallace Stevens' between your title and the start of your poem. This is called an epigraph.

My House of Many Moods

My House of Many Moods
In my dining room of boredom,
the dining room table is made of factual books.
The dinner plates are covered in chat shows.
The table cloth is made from school.

In my garage of jealousy,
the car runs on beautiful things that my best friends have.
My work bench is made of a Ferrari Testarossa.
The oil can squirts out the football team that I'm not in.

James (extract)

Now it's your turn. Be sure you read all the details below before you start writing.

✳ We all have our moods! Some good and positive, some bad and negative. Begin with noting down at least two of your moods – maybe one good, one bad. To help you think, here are some suggestions:

Positive moods: friendliness, excitement, energy, calm, helpfulness, cheerfulness.
Negative moods: laziness, envy, frustration, grumpiness, stress, sadness.

✳ Choose your moods from these or from your own ideas about yourself.

✳ Now make some notes:

1. For each mood, write down a room. For example: cheerfulness – kitchen.

2. Write two or three things that get you in this mood. For example: sunshine, friends, favourite comedian.

3. Write things found in your room that will act as symbols for the mood, for example: oven, mugs, kettle.

✳ Now write an opening line with the room and the mood as James did.

✳ Finally, look back at lines 2–4 of James' poem to see how he wove all his details into the lines – and write your own.

My Magic Paintbrush

My Magic Paintbrush

If I have a magic paintbrush, I will paint Gary Barlow for my mum.
I will paint for my dad children who always do what he says.
I will paint for my little sister Willy Wonka and his chocolate factory.
I will paint every computer game in the world for my cousin James.
And last, I will paint for my grandad, good health.

Joe

Now it is your turn…

First, read all the details below before you start your writing.

✳ There's a very old Chinese story about a young boy who is given a paintbrush. The boy is told that whatever he paints will become real. However, he must only paint things for other people, things these people really need, things that will make their lives better.

✳ If you had such a brush, what would you paint?

✳ You can paint things for members of your family, your friends, adults you know well. What different things would each person need and love to have?

✳ Your ideas can be serious or funny – or better still, both!

✳ Write one idea for every person you choose.

✳ You can begin your writing like Joe did if you wish.

Welcome to Planet X

Welcome to Planet X

Where the moon shines by day and the sun comes out at night.
Where trees grow underground with only their roots in the air.
Where cars run on chocolate ice cream.
Where babies can speak as soon as they are born
       and every grown up speaks 50 languages.
Where rain tastes like apple juice
    and everyone loves sprouts!

             Adam

Now it's your turn…

First, read all the details below before you start your writing.

✱ Write the title at the top of your page.

✱ Life on Planet X is just like life here on Earth – and also completely different. Planet X has all the things and features we have here – only there, they are the exact opposite.

✱ Begin each line, 'Where' and then say how something on Planet X is so very different.

✱ You can put more than one idea into a single line if you want.

✱ Write as many lines as you have time for. Here are some ideas for lines to get you started:

Buildings, the weather, animals, the oceans, transport, clothing, food, computers, the landscape, toys, the jobs Planet X people do.

Cracking Creative Writing by David Horner © Brilliant Publications Limited. *This page may be copied by the purchasing institution only.*

On a Magic Carpet

On a Magic Carpet

We will go around the world four times in a day. Then we can visit my cousins in Birmingham. We will ski over the Antarctic. Next the carpet will take us to New Zealand.
We will go under the ocean and see sharks and afterwards we will walk on Saturn's rings.

Michael and Jack

Now it is your turn.

First, read all the details below before you start your writing.

✳ Write the title at the top of your paper.

✳ You are going to take someone with you on some very exciting journeys on this carpet.

✳ Here are some possible journeys:

To visit friends or family far away
To watch some wild animals
To a foreign country or city
To the North or South Pole
Under the sea
Into outer space
Back in time or forwards in time

✳ You can start each journey on a new line if you wish. Aim to describe five or six journeys.

✳ Here are some ways of introducing each journey:

We will go
We can travel
We will fly

✳ Can you think of a different beginning for each journey?

✳ Look back at how Michael and Jack begin their sentences if it helps you.

✳ You can finish by writing what you will do when you are safely back home!

Spot the Difference

How to Tell a Banana from a Bicycle

You can't keep a bicycle in a fruit bowl.
Bananas don't have wheels and a saddle.
You don't have to learn to ride a banana.
A bicycle isn't a fruit.
A bicycle won't turn black if you leave it in a fridge for a week.
Bicycle and banana begin with the same letter and go on with different ones.
No-one has ever won the Tour de France on a banana.
You can't add a bicycle to a curry.
You can't fall off a banana.
You cannot slip on a bicycle skin.

Annabel, Vanya and Libby

This idea comes from a poem by John Hegley, called 'The Differences between Dogs and Deckchairs'.

Now it's your turn. Be sure you read all the details below before you start writing.

✳ Choose your two items for spotting differences.

✳ Make the objects as unalike and different from one another as you can. So maybe not a pen and a pencil, but a pen and a double decker bus or a pencil and a tent might work well.

✳ Write quickly. Don't plan the order of your ideas; just write whatever differences come to you. The more obvious the differences, the more humorous your poem becomes.

✳ You don't have to keep all your ideas in your final collection, just the ones you feel work well. However, if you feel they all work well, then keep them – and well done you!

Two Halves Make a Whole

> **It is warm and quiet in the library.**
> Come on, Mrs Reilly. Where are you?
> **It's another cold February day outside.**
> I knock on her office door, where she might be working.
> **In the library, keyboards are getting clicked; pages are getting turned.**
> Once again, I knock on her door; she tells me to wait.
> **I can sniff the usual smell of school dinners.**
> Opening the door slowly, I see that Mrs Reilly is dressed as Wonder Woman.
>
> *Rebecca*

Now it's your turn. Be sure you read all the details below before you start writing.

✳ You are going to write a whole piece in two halves. It will make either a complete piece, like Rebecca's, or possibly the beginning of a novel!

✳ Begin by choosing an ordinary scene: a beach, a street, the doctor's waiting room, wherever you are right now.

✳ Something very unusual is going to happen in your ordinary scene: a pirate ship appears out at sea from your beach; a huge storm builds above your street; a clown enters the waiting room; you see a UFO descending outside where you are now.

✳ You can choose one of these ideas or one of your own. What you have to do is create a complete contrast between that ordinary scene and the extraordinary event that unfolds.

✳ First, write between four to six double spaced lines, describing your ordinary scene: say what it is, its appearance and atmosphere; describe the weather, the time, the season; describe a detail or two – a smell, a sound, people around you. Keep it ordinary, and write in ordinary, straightforward sentences – in either the past or the present tense.

✳ Now – in the spaces between these lines – create the slowly developing extraordinary event. Remember to write in the same tense as the other lines.

✳ To make the event feel more extraordinary and dramatic, write unusual sentences. Here are some suggestions:

Write a very short sentence – three words maximum.
Include a simile or metaphor in a sentence.
Write a sentence using a passive verb.
End a sentence with a question mark.
Include some direct speech.
Include an ellipsis or a colon.

✳ Rebecca used some of these devices. Look back and work out which ones.

 Cracking Creative Writing by David Horner © Brilliant Publications Limited. *This page may be copied by the purchasing institution only.*

If...

IF...

If I was invisible, I would live in a tree all day and all night.
I would go under the seas and oceans to the centre of the earth.
I would visit the Queen without mum and dad.
We have a wa-wa-wa-ing baby
and I would hide from it till next day.

Lloyd

Now it's your turn.

First, read all the details below before you start your writing.

✻ What super power would you choose? To be invisible? To have wings and be able to fly? To grow really tall? To have x-ray eyes?

✻ You can only have one magical ability. You can choose from the ideas above or use an idea of your own.

✻ Now, here's a reminder of the five senses: taste, touch, sight, sound and smell.

✻ You are going to write a poem, explaining what you would do with your new power, using each one of your senses in turn.

✻ First, write that title at the top of your page. Don't forget the ellipsis.

✻ Begin your writing with 'If I' and write what your chosen super power is.

✻ Now, work through the senses in turn. You decide the order of your lines. You choose your 'sensing' verb each time.

✻ So your poem will be set out something like this:

> *If I + your chosen new power*
> *I would taste… Or eat. Or drink. Or…*
> *I would touch… Or feel. Or hold. Or…*
> *I would see… Or watch. Or stare at. Or...*
> *I would hear… Or listen to. Or tune into. Or…*
> *I would smell… Or breathe in. Or sniff. Or…*

When I Am –

When I Am –

When I am the sun, I will shine on all the world.
When I am the moon, I will light up the jet-black sky.
When I am a comet, I will shoot past the roof tops.
When I am a star, I will let you wish upon me.
When I am the sky, I will be blue for ever.

Jessica and Adam

Now it is your turn.

✳ Put the title at the top of your page. Don't forget the dash!

First, read all the details below before you start your writing.

✳ Imagine you can become things in outer space! What will you choose to be – the Moon, a star, an asteroid, the Milky Way? And what will you do?

✳ Put each idea on a new line. Aim to write five or six lines.

✳ For every idea, begin 'When I am…'. Next, write what you have decided to be. And finally write what you will now do.

✳ Is there an encyclopaedia about space in school, to help you with ideas?

 Cracking Creative Writing by David Horner © Brilliant Publications Limited. This page may be copied by the purchasing institution only.

No, No, No, November!

> No sun—no moon!
>   No morn—no noon—
> No dawn—no dusk—no proper time of day—
>   No sky—no earthly view—
> No distance looking blue—

Those lines are the opening of a poem by Thomas Hood (1799 – 1845). Here is how the poem ends:

> No shade, no shine, no butterflies, no bees,
> No fruits, no flowers, no leaves, no birds
>
> November!

Thomas Hood lived in Victorian London and he probably wrote the poem to show how grim life could be in a city, so often buried under industrial fog and smog.

Now it's your turn. Be sure you read all the details below before you start writing.

✱ This poem is still well known and popular today – when we no longer suffer nineteenth century winter smog. This is because, more than 150 years later, we read the piece differently. The endless complaining feels almost comically exaggerated. But we still recognise the bad mood the poet is in and, like him, we all have our own Novembers.

✱ So, what will you have in your November? What would you miss? Think of all the things that make your life enjoyable and satisfying – people, events, festivals, weather, films, foods, pets – in fact everything and everybody that matter to you.

✱ Write your things down just in the order they come to you – and add that word No before each.

✱ Put between one and three things on each line of your writing. Have a mixture of line lengths as this will make your poem feel more immediate and dramatic.

✱ Don't forget to finish your poem with the key word – November!

✱ Of course, there's always Bonfire Night! Maybe you or someone known to you has a birthday in November? Perhaps you have a special event in November? If so, you can use any of them for a last line. The sudden contrast will totally transform the mood of your piece.

✱ Hood's poem has come to be known by two titles – 'No!' and 'November'. Choose either of these for your title.

It's a Crazy, Mixed up World...

It's a Crazy, Mixed up World...

where
dogs ring, '**Ding dong, ding dong**,'
where the thunder hisses,
where cuckoos roar like fire-breathing dragons,
where buses sing pop songs all day long,
where babies go '**Woof!**' in their cots,
where snakes go, '**Googoogoo**,'
where doorbells rumble
and window cleaners sing, '**Cuckoo! Cuckoo!**'

Louis and John

The idea for this activity comes from Charles Causley's poem "Quack!' said the Billy-Goat'. The poem features lots of animals, all making the wrong noise, such as a hen that oinks, a cow that baas and a sheep that goes 'Cock-a-doodle-doo!'

Now it's your turn. Be sure you read all the details below before you start writing.

✳ Charles Causley included only farm animals in his poem. You are going to go take the craziness a step further to include sounds from anywhere – pets; more farm animals; wild animals from land, sea and air; machines and engines; the weather; different languages. The whole world is there for you.

✳ Begin by noting down at least six things that make a sound – more if you like. The most important thing is to make your collection as varied as possible in order to create your world of noises.

✳ Beside your noise-makers add the noise each makes.

✳ Next, draw lines from each noise-maker to each noise, so that every noise-maker gets a wrong noise.

✳ Write the title, 'It's a Crazy Mixed up World…' at the top of your page and underneath write the word where.

✳ Now you write the lines of your poem in any order that pleases you.

✳ Hint: Add details to some of your lines to bring them fully to life.

Some Curious Cures

Some Curious Cures

To cure asthma, rub goose grease on your chest and cover it with brown paper.
For the toothache, run around a church clockwise, taking care not to think of a fox.
If you have tonsillitis, sit with a poached egg on your head, roasted onions around your neck,
                                        and have a red herbal powder blown into your mouth.
To recover from malaria, swallow a spider wrapped in a raisin.
For baldness, sleep on stones.   *Traditional remedies*

Strange but true, these 'cures' – and many like them – were once used by people who believed they would really work. Maybe sometimes they did…

Now it's your turn…

First, read all the details below before you start your writing.

✳   Write the title at the top of your page.

✳   Now make up some weird and wonderful cures of your own, just like the ones you've now read.

✳   Begin by choosing some of the illnesses and accidents we all get these days – tummy ache, sore throats, hay fever, bumps on the head, for example – and for each one come up with a cure.

✳   To get started, use the openings 'To cure…', 'For…', 'If you have…', as in the examples above – or openings you can think of yourself. Then once you've named the illness or accident, make the cure as wonderfully bizarre and richly detailed as you can.

26 Letters – 26 Words

See How They Move

Awesome bears crazily dance.
Emerald frogs go hopping in joyful kicks.
Ladybirds move neatly over petals.
Quiet reindeer slowly twist up valleys,
while excited yaks zigzag.

Francesca

Now it's your turn.

Be sure you read all the details below before you start writing.

✳ Looks easy, eh? Just 26 words to write – and each just has to begin with the letters of the alphabet in the correct order.

✳ Well, be careful, it's not as easy as it looks! Here are some tips for you:

✳ You haven't got a lot to write, so be ready to spend time changing your mind and crossing out one word for another. That's the fun of this activity.

✳ Don't worry if what you write doesn't make perfect sense. Enjoy where your ideas take you.

✳ If you finish with a truly crazy piece, well just enjoy its craziness!

✳ You can write sentences of one word or just one sentence of 26 words – and every length of sentence in between.

✳ The second half of the alphabet is harder to play with than the first. Have a dictionary ready for some necessary word-hunting.

✳ The letter X is especially tough. Francesca went for a word that sounds right but begins 'ex'. You can do this too, if you like.

✳ Instead of, or as well as, a poem, you can also try writing a 26-word opening to a story with the same A-Z rule.

 Cracking Creative Writing by David Horner © Brilliant Publications Limited. This page may be copied by the purchasing institution only.

Name that Band!

Name that Band!

The Aeronautical Bananas

The Curious Demons

The Electric Feathers
Extract from class piece

Now it's your turn.

Read all the details below before you start writing.

✴ Imagine you have heard a brand-new pop band. They sound great, they look great, their songs are great – they will be great! The only thing they don't have is a great band name.

✴ This is where you come in: the band has asked you to come up with some possible names for them.

✴ They need 13 names altogether to choose one from. This is the pattern they have given you:

The + adjective + noun

✴ The adjective and noun must follow the sequence *A-B, C-D, E-F, G-H,* etc. as in the extract above, all the way to *Y-Z.*

✴ The band want a very unusual name for themselves, so do your very best to find the weirdest, most unlikely pairings of adjective and nouns you can. Don't be afraid to be different!

The Great Word Hunt

The Great Word Hunt

A is alarmingly angry.
B is brilliantly beautiful.
C is colourfully clever.
D is definitely dippy.
E is easily excited.

Victoria and Jake (extract)

Now it's your turn.

First, read all the details below before you start your writing.

✳ Write the title at the top of your page.

✳ Down the left side of the page write the letters of the alphabet and add the word 'is' after each letter.

✳ Before you start your writing, be sure you have the writer's best friend with you – a dictionary!

✳ You are going on a word hunt. For each letter of the alphabet you are looking for two adjectives – the best, the most interesting, unusual, exciting ones you can find in your dictionary. Maybe adjectives you have never come across before.

✳ To be sure a word is an adjective, check that your dictionary has '*adj*' after the word.

✳ Decide which adjective will go first and which will go second for each letter and now make the first adjective into an adverb simply by adding '-ly' to the end of your first one. So, for example, 'amazing' becomes 'amazingly', 'bold' becomes 'boldly', 'cool' becomes 'coolly'.

✳ Try swapping the order of your words round each time and say them to yourself, to see which order you prefer.

✳ When you reach X, don't panic! Go back in your dictionary and look for two adjectives starting 'ex.'

Round the World in 26 Letters

Round the World in 26 Letters

A is an artist acting amazingly in Athens.
B is a butcher building a bathroom badly in Beijing.
C is a cook catching crabs carefully in Copenhagen.
D is a dentist dancing dangerously in Detroit.

Extract from a class-made alphabet

Now it's your turn. You need a dictionary, a thesaurus and an atlas.

Read all the details below before you start writing.

✳ Now write the title at the top of your page.

✳ Look at the extract above and you will quickly see the pattern of the lines.

✳ Each time you tackle a letter of the alphabet, follow these steps:

 • Write the capital letter followed by the word 'is'.

 • Choose a person's job or occupation that starts with this letter. Your dictionary and thesaurus can help you here.

 • Next add a verb that starts with this letter. Use your dictionary to help you find a verb you like. Write it in the progressive form – ending in '-ing'.

 • Now you need an adverb that starts with this letter.

 • You might find adjectives first of all and you can usually add '-ly' to the end to make the adverb.

 • Finally, write 'in' and finish the line with a city or country that starts with this letter. Use your atlas to find these places.

✳ Work quickly but don't rush to finish. This is a piece you can always come back to.

✳ **Hint:** When you reach X, don't panic! Use 'ex' to begin your key words.

The Most Mysterious Martian Alphabet

A is for paint
B is for heel
C is for quaint
D is for zeal

E is for lad
F is for sock
G is for bad
H is for knock

Sarah (extract)

Breaking News! A robotic digger on Mars has discovered examples of Martian writing – buried in the red dust for millions of years. Amazingly, Martians spoke and wrote English! However, although they used our alphabet, none of the 26 written letters match our letter sounds. You can clearly see this in Sarah's example above.

And now it's your turn.

✳ First, write the alphabet in six groups of four letters down the left side of your page: ABCD, EFGH, etc. Finish by writing underneath the last two letters – Y and Z – as a pair.

✳ After each letter, just add the phrase 'is for.'

✳ You now have the beginnings to six four-line verses, called **quatrains**, and one two-line verse, called a **couplet**.

✳ Now start to complete each quatrain. The rules are: lines 1 and 3 must rhyme, and lines 2 and 4 must rhyme, and the rhyming words you choose must NOT begin with the correct English letter. Have your dictionary handy!

✳ Look back to Sarah's opening verses to see what she did. To complete your Martian Alphabet, the words of that final couplet must make a single final rhyme.

✳ To put even more comedy into your rhymes, add some alliteration. So, Sarah's second verse could become:

E is for a lazy lad
F is for a very smelly sock
G is for both bonkers and bad
H is for some knees that knock

✳ The famous Beatle, John Lennon, wrote a Martian alphabet. It begins, 'A is for parrot'.

✳ As an extra challenge, can you write your alphabet using each letter only once at the start of your rhyming words? If you try this, use the difficult letters such as Q, X and Z early. Tick off the letters as you use them.

Countdown!

COUNTDOWN!

10 colourfully crazy cards
9 sensationally super surprises
8 groovily gorgeous greetings
7 terrifically tremendous treats
6 brilliantly bright balloons
5 really red ribbons
4 famously foolish friends
3 teasingly tiny texts
2 fantastically far-out phone calls
1 perfectly playful party
0 – it's my birthday!

Tasmin and Jordi

This kind of writing is called occasional writing – writing done for a particular occasion or event. In the example above, it's a birthday. But you can choose any occasion, for example, the end of a school term, Christmas, Diwali, Eid, springtime, bonfire night, the weekend. Any event where counting down to it builds excitement and anticipation.

And now it's your turn. First choose your occasion and note down ten things that are connected to your occasion.

✴ To make your writing more varied, see if you can make your chosen things start with different letters. Look back at Tasmin and Jordi's piece to see how they almost managed it.

✴ Write the numbers 10 to 0 down the left side of a clean page.

✴ Down the right side of the page – on the same lines as the numbers – write your 10 chosen things. Be sure to leave lots of space between the numbers and the things.

✴ Now, using your dictionary, find two different adjectives and write them between each of the ten numbers and things. Each pair of adjectives must begin with the same letter sound as the thing they are now describing. Your dictionary should help you – if it has 'adj' after a word, then it's an adjective.

✴ Change the first adjective to an adverb by adding '-ly' to the end of the word. So, for example, Tasmin and Jordi found colourful and crazy and then added '-ly' to the one they wanted first. Try swapping the order of each pair of adjectives to see which way you prefer.

✴ Finally, after the zero, write your chosen occasion.

Twice Upon a Time...

Twice Upon a Time...

We saw
    One omnipotent octopus ogling.
      Two terrestrial teapots tapdancing.
        Three theatrical thingumajigs throwing.
          Four fiery fishcakes flirting.
            Five fabulous farmers following.
              Six seasick sailors sword-swallowing.
                Ryan and Danny (extract)

Now it's your turn. Be sure you read all the details below before you start writing. You need a dictionary.

* You are about to create some mouth music, a piece of alliterating madness that will astound your readers with its verbal trickery!

* Write the title at the top of your page, plus the ellipsis, to show that more is to come.

* Ryan and Danny then began their piece, 'We saw.' You can do the same, or write something similar, with an introductory phrase such as 'I met,' 'I came across,' 'I went partying with'.

* Down the left side of your page write the numbers one to ten. Write these as words to establish the key alliterative (repeated) letter sounds from the start.

* For each number, you now need an adjective, a noun and a verb. This is where you need that dictionary. Open it at each key letter sound (o, t, th, f, etc.) and go on a great word hunt! Be adventurous. Find words you've never used or even met before.

* Before you write them down, just check in your dictionary that the words you choose each time are an adjective, a noun and a verb.

* The more outlandish your chosen words, the better the nonsense and the more your readers will be impressed by your vocabulary and verbal skills.

* **Hint 1**: Remember to make all the nouns from two to ten plural.

* **Hint 2**: Don't forget to write the verb in its progressive form each time, by adding '-ing' to the verb. This is important, so that each line makes good grammatical sense as well as being quite perfect nonsense!

A Counting Song

A Counting Song

One *is an old, orange oven.*
Two *is a tiny, tingling teapot.*
Three *is a thrilling, thin throne.*
Four *is a funny, famous flapjack.*
Five *is a fine, flying foot.*

Stefan

Now it's your turn… Make sure you have a dictionary with you.

First, read all the details below before you start your writing.

✳ Write the title at the top of your page.

✳ Fold your page in half lengthwise. Fold your page in half again. Open the page back out and you have four columns going down the page.

✳ In the first column write the opening, 'One is an'.

✳ Columns 2 and 3 are for two adjectives. They must both begin with 'o' – and so now go adjective hunting! Open your dictionary at 'o' to find the two most exciting adjectives you can. If a word is an adjective, your dictionary will say so by having '*adj*' after the word.

✳ When you have found your two adjectives, write one in Column 2 and one in Column 3.

✳ Column 4 is for a noun. In this first line, it too must begin with 'o'. Look in your dictionary again and find your noun. Again, look for something unusual to finish your first alliterating line strongly.

✳ You are ready now for your second line – so write, 'Two is a'; find two alliterating adjectives and one alliterating noun; and write all three words in their spaces across the page.

✳ Aim to complete five lines at least – and ten if you can.

✳ **Hints:**
  • Don't forget you need a comma between the adjectives in each line, and don't forget your full stop at the end of each line.
  • Most lines in your song have the phrase 'is a' after the number. Line 1, though, had 'One is an', because the number starts with a vowel. What is the next number where you'll have to write 'an' rather than 'a'?

✳ Be careful but, above all, be interesting!

The Song of the Sums

The Song of the Sums

2 ÷ 6
is a magician who has no tricks.
9 x 3
is a performing circus flea.
1 - 8
is an early train that's always late.

Phill (extract)

Here's a way to do some writing and some sums, both at the same time! Be sure you read all the details below before you start writing.

✳ Write the title at the top of your page and then, down the left side, write the numbers 1 to 10. You can write them as digits or words and you can write them in either the correct or a jumbled order.

✳ After each number write any one of the arithmetic symbols, +, -, x, ÷.

✳ After each symbol, write the numbers 1-10, again in the correct or a jumbled order. Check you haven't repeated a number or left any out.

✳ One of the interesting features of the numbers 1 to 10, is that no two numbers rhyme. They all have a different sound, and this give us lots of rhyming material for our songs of the sums.

✳ Remember, it's the second number you need to rhyme with. As in Phill's 6/tricks, 3/flea, 8/late.

✳ It might help you to begin your rhymes by noting down rhyme words you can think of for each number. When you have ones you like, compose the song line to get to your rhyme word. You can have slightly sad rhymes; clever ones like Phill's; extremely silly ones; or a thoroughly enjoyable mixture!

✳ **Hint:** As well as the rhyme, your pairs of lines need their rhythm. This comes from their stressed and unstressed syllables. Basically, you need at least two stressed syllables in each line. For example:

2 x 7
is a **day** in ***Dev***on

✳ Phill's first lines have the same two stresses but the rhyme line can then have as many as four stresses, as here: **1 - 8** / is an **early train** that's **always late**. Just say, or sing, your lines to yourself a few times until you're happy with their music.

 Cracking Creative Writing by David Horner © Brilliant Publications Limited. This page may be copied by the purchasing institution only.

Crazy Space!

Crazy Space!

On Mercury the milkmen make marmalade.
   On Venus the vets vanish in Volvos.
On Earth eggs are expensive everywhere.
   On Mars magicians make monsters into mind readers.
On Jupiter all the jugglers juggle jam.
   On Saturn swordfish swim in soup.
On Uranus umbrellas are usually upside down.
   On Neptune the nurses nick other people's knickers.

Stefanie

Now it is your turn.

First, read all the details below before you start your writing.

✱ Write the title at the top of your paper.

✱ Write 'On' eight times down the left side of your page, leaving a line or two empty each time, so that your writing won't get all squashed up.

✱ Write the names of the planets after each 'On':

   Mercury, Venus, Earth, Mars, Jupiter, Saturn, Uranus, Neptune.

✱ Take the first letter of each planet and complete eight alliterating lines. The crazier the line, the better! How many alliterating words can you cram into each line?

✱ Get a dictionary to help with all the word hunting.

✱ If you have time, you can put 'On Pluto' on a new line and write one more line for that tiny, one-time planet.

The Alliteration Relations

The Alliteration Relations

Sister Susie is sewing shirts for soldiers.
Brother Billy is baking bread for builders.
Auntie Anne is arranging apples for architects.
Uncle Uri is unfastening umbrellas for undertakers.
Daddy Danny is driving diggers for dentists.
Great Grandma Gwendolyn is getting glasses for gardeners.
And Sister Susie is still sewing shirts for soldiers.

Danny and Alex

The first line of the piece above is a very well-known tongue twister. Try repeating it a few times to get the rhythm and pattern of the line fixed for yourself.

Tongue twisters are built around what is called in a poem **alliteration**: the repetition of the same letter sound at the start of words. That's what makes them hard – and fun – to say!

Now it's your turn. Be sure you read all the details below before you start writing.

* The challenge here is to write more tongue twisters that copy the structure and pattern of the original.

* On your page, write the title, and underneath, write that original tongue twister.

* Down the left of the page, one under the other, write a list of six to eight different family members. Use any in Alex and Danny's collection and add more you have thought of.

* After each family member, add an alliterating first name.

* Write 'is' followed by the main verb. Again, it must alliterate and be in the progressive form – with an -'ing' ending.

* Next you need an alliterating object to follow the verb. So, Danny and Alex had 'baking bread' and 'driving diggers'.

* Write 'for' and then write an alliterating adult – in the job they do.

* Danny and Alex finished by (almost) repeating the first line. You can do the same if you wish. This is called a frame to a piece of writing.

From Me – To You

I am pizza and chips.
I am rain and a cat.
I am chocolate cake.
I am Alton Towers.
    I am a sparkling pink dress.

You are cold custard.
You are fog.
You are black tea.
You are town in the dark.
    You are tight black pants.

Gemma

Now it is your turn.

First, read all the details below before you start your writing.

✳ Write a list of five or six things you like a lot. Aim for five or six very different ideas, so not five or six foods but just one food, then maybe the weather, animals, music, colours, a time of day. You choose!

✳ There's no need to write a sentence, just the item is enough. But do write each of your likes on a new line.

✳ Now write a list of five or six things you definitely don't like – using the same subjects as your likes. Again, write just the item, each on a new line.

✳ Now write the phrase 'I am' before the items in the first list and write the phrase 'You are' before the items in the second list.

✳ Do feel free now to add details to your items – adjectives perhaps – to bring each line fully to life.

Better than the Bee's Knees!

Better than the Bee's Knees

You are the leopard's spots.
You're the shark's fin,
and the zebra's stripes.

You are the parrot's shriek.
You're the cat's purr,
and the donkey's hee-haw.

You are the tadpole's teapot.
You're the bullfrog's beard,
and the crocodile's cuddle.

Jake, Hannah and Tamsin

When we say someone, or something, is 'the bee's knees', we just mean they are the very, very best. Another phrase like it is, 'the cat's whiskers'. Sometimes also, 'the cat's pyjamas'!

And now it's your turn. You are going to make up some more.

First, read all the details below before you start your writing.

✳ Write the title at the top of your page.

✳ Now all you have to do is choose your animals. Choose a wide range: insects, large animals, flying creatures, sea creatures, even extinct ones.

✳ Choose animals with unusual colours; ones with features that make them stand out; ones with very distinctive voices.

✳ Or, you might give your animals wackier features, as in the last verse of the poem above. Or some impossible ones – snake's legs, octopus's wings.

✳ You can write a simple collection of animals and features in the time you have.

✳ Or, you can make some short verses, again like the poem above.

✳ You might even write a whole Bee's Knees Alliterating Alphabet, beginning like this:

You are the alligator's advertisement.
You are the bluebottle's beard.
You are the crow's candy floss.

The Flavours of the Days

Monday tastes of Cubs after tea.
Tuesday tastes of homework to be handed in.
Wednesday tastes of football training with everyone.
Thursday tastes of going round Tesco with mum and a big trolley.
Friday tastes of a test and a weekend coming.
Saturday tastes of Match of the Day.
Sunday tastes of a very big lunch!

Ali

Now it is your turn.

First, read all the details below before you start your writing.

✳ Write the title at the top of your page.

✳ What do your days taste of? Think of each day in turn and choose one important thing that makes that day different to the others – and write it down.

✳ One tip is to write the days down your page first – and don't worry about writing your tastes in order. Just add your chosen things to each day as and when you think of them.

The Many Moods of the Months

The Many Moods of the Months

January is mean and nasty, with cold hands.
February is a bad-tempered bully.
March is wild and very mischievous.
April is shy but will smile sometimes.

Siobhan and Brendon (extract)

Now it's your turn.

First, read all the details below before you start your writing.

✳ Write the title at the top of your page.

✳ Write the names of the twelve months down the left side. Check your spellings!

✳ If each of these months was a person, how would they act? What would their behaviour, emotions and moods be?

✳ This idea is called **personification**. If you are going to successfully make twelve different, individual persons, then the moods of each month must be clearly different.

✳ A thesaurus might be a big help here. If you can't think of the exact word you want, look up one like it, and choose a good one from all the words on offer.

✳ **Hint:** Don't feel you have to work down your months in order. See which ones suggest their moods quickest to you and do them first. Then go back to the ones you've missed out.

✳ Always feel you can go back and change your first ideas.

A Day in the Life of...

> **A Day in the Life of a Football Stadium**
>
> *Saturday, March 8.* I woke early. I always do on Saturdays. It rained in the morning and a few humans arrived. They cut my grass and painted those white lines on me. I looked so smart. But ooh, it tickled. In the afternoon thousands of humans came inside me! I felt so full. I thought I would burst! And the noise they made! At 3 o'clock a few more humans ran all over my grass in coloured shirts. Then at 5 o'clock all the humans disappeared, and I was on my own again. It was very, very quiet all night.
>
> *Martha*

Early on July 31st, 1802, William Wordsworth stood on Westminster Bridge, over the River Thames in London, and wrote his famous poem. In it, he sees London wearing the dawn light like a garment. And in the quiet of the morning he senses that 'all that mighty heart is lying still'.

Wordsworth is clearly imagining London as a living place. Well, what if the city is alive and can speak for itself? What if all other places can? What if they can write? What if a place keeps a diary?

A diary is where we record not just what happens in a day, but also our private thoughts, feelings and secrets.

You are going to write a diary entry for one day in the life of one place. Be sure you read all the details below before you start writing.

✳ First, choose your place. Any place. For example, an ocean, a shed, Saturn, a playground, the Leaning Tower of Pisa, an iceberg.

✳ Write the title, 'A Day in the Life of' and add the place you have chosen.

✳ Next, choose a date for your place's diary entry. If possible, a date in an interesting time for the place. For example, Christmas Day in a house, Midsummer's Day in Blackpool, a spring day in a forest.

✳ Now think about your chosen place and note down anything you think might happen there on the day you've chosen. Most importantly, think how the place feels about the events of the day. What excites it, what annoys it, what puzzles it. Think so hard, you start to become the place.

✳ Write the date you've picked and now write the diary entry.

✳ **Hint:** A good way to show straight away that you are imagining yourself as the place is to begin with the first-person pronoun 'I'.

Tonight at Noon

On February 31st 2099,
rain will make us dry and warm,
dinosaurs will be spotted at the equator,
Santa Claus will leave presents for grown ups
and I will get a Merit in my music exam.

On February 31st 2099,
the school bus will stop right outside my door,
beggars and millionaires will swap places,
chips and crisps and chocolate will be very healthy for us to eat,
and my brother will help me every day with my homework.

Tara

'Tonight at Noon' is the title of the first poem in *The Mersey Sound,* first published in 1967, with poems by Adrian Henri, Brian Patten and Roger McGough. It has sold over half a million copies.

The poem itself was written by Adrian Henri, who starts it with that impossible time and then goes on to list lots more impossibilities, mixing the serious and the comic. For example, America will declare peace on Russia and pigeons will hunt cats through city backyards. The end of the poem is both personal and touching:

And
You will tell me you love me
Tonight at noon.

Now it's your turn. Be sure you read all the details below before you start writing.

✳   You can use Adrian Henri's title – he borrowed it from a jazz record himself – or make up your own impossible time or date, as Tara did in her poem.

✳   This title then gives you your opening line. Follow this with your own variety of impossibilities and contradictions. Aim for a range of ideas, from the funny and light-hearted to the dark and serious.

✳   You can write all your ideas as one long poem or break them into short verses as Tara did.

✳   Finish your poem or each small verse with an issue that is important to you, something personal, something you would really like to happen. Added to all the other impossibilities, this gives your poem a real emotional range.

Yesterday, Today and Tomorrow

Yesterday, Today and Tomorrow

Yesterday I was Zac.

However, today I am a full bag of bacon crisps.
I am a pair of unwashed socks.
I am Homer Simpson.
I am a crater on the dark side of the moon.
I am New Year's Eve.
And tomorrow I will be a sabre tooth tiger in my forest.

Zac

Now it is your turn.

First, read all the details below before you start your writing.

✻ First write the title.

✻ Underneath, write the phrase, 'Yesterday I was' and then your name. Just your first name or your full name. You choose!

✻ On a new line, write the phrase, 'However, today I am...'

✻ Now change yourself into five or six different things. Aim for lots of variety in the things you choose, and add details to each one, as in Zac's poem.

✻ Write each idea on a new line, beginning each, 'I am'.

✻ Finally, on the last line, write the phrase, 'And tomorrow I will be' and finish the line by changing yourself into any wild animal, anywhere in the world. (Not your little brother!)

A Beginner's Guide

How to Write a Masterpiece

You need a sharpened pencil and one sheet of white paper. Hold your pencil with the thumb, forefinger and middle finger of your normal writing hand and keep the paper still by spreading the fingers of your free hand across it. The pencil must have the point down.

The paper will feel cool under your hand. Gently put the pencil point to the paper and begin to write. Lift the pencil a little from the paper after every word and bit of punctuation. Read what you have written.

Kristian

It's obviously important to be able to give instructions and to understand them. For example: directions to your house; a recipe; the rules of a game. They must be short, simple, clear. The simpler the task, the simpler the instructions. So, to make a sandwich, we get told to use a knife to spread the butter. To wash our hands, we are asked to begin by rinsing our hands in water.

But they don't say how to hold the knife, what the butter looks like as it spreads over the bread, what smells may arise. They don't tell us the sound of the water coming from the tap, how to move our hands under the water, how the water feels on our skin.

Instructions just want to get their job done. They don't try to be interesting. But that doesn't mean they can't be!

Now it's your turn. Be sure you read all the details below before you start writing.

✳ As you will be writing in much greater depth and detail than in normal instructions, you must choose a very, very simple task – something your readers will assume they know already and therefore don't need instructions for. Your job is to open their eyes to make them see the obvious in a new light.

✳ Choose one of the instructions ideas below – or think of one for yourself:

How to pour a glass of lemonade
How to scratch your nose
How to stroke a dog
How to open a door
How to smile

✳ Begin by jotting down the simple steps of your chosen task as a draft. Try to imagine the task over and over until you get the feel, taste, smell, sound and look of it all. Now begin!

Unique You

A Recipe to Make a Cool Elizabeth

Take ¼ tin of Top of the Pops
a drop of jeans, T-shirt and other things
a litre of bedroom and England
a jug of playing with my friends
5 bowls of wishing to see my best friend in Australia

Stir in – a dollop of happiness and laziness
a tablespoon of long titian hair and hazel eyes

Cook for – 10 years in Jersey.

Serve – with SPICE GIRLS IN LONDON.

Now it's your turn. Be sure you read all the details below before you start writing.

✳ In 1818 Mary Shelley, aged just 20, published *Frankenstein*. In the story, Dr Frankenstein creates his monster as an experiment and successfully brings it to life. Well, you're not making a monster, but you are going to make yourself a unique individual. Here's how.

✳ Note down a collection of the people and things that matter most to you, for example: family members, friends, pets, places, music, games, activities, ambitions for the future.

✳ That list is your ingredients. Decide how much of each one your recipe needs and as Elizabeth did, list one under the other, each with a quantity.

✳ Next, stir in some of the things that make you you: your moods, habits, appearance, quirky ways.

✳ Next you need to say how long you will need in the oven! Elizabeth had spent all her first ten years in one place. What place or places have you lived in – and for how long? See if you can have a fresh 'cooking' verb for each period of time.

✳ Decide where you wish to be served. The world is your restaurant!

✳ Finally, make up your own title – like Elizabeth's, but with the adjective that fits you best.

A Recipe to Make a Story

A packet of characters
Two sachets of exciting plot
A large can of a good beginning
Five boxes of full stops
A family size carton of a great ending
One bowl of illustrations
Three whole bags full of words
Six jugs of suspense

Ivan and Liam

Now it's your turn. Be sure you read all the details below before you start writing. Have a thesaurus handy.

✳ You are going to write a recipe for one of these subjects:

a poem   a playscript   a joke book   a picture book   an atlas   a dictionary   a comic
an encyclopaedia   a graphic novel   a thesaurus

✳ When you have chosen your subject, note down all the different ingredients that must go into it. Aim for six or more.

✳ When you have your ingredients, make a short list of containers – boxes, bottles, baskets – one for each of your ingredients. You can research ideas in your thesaurus here.

✳ Now, just put one container together with one ingredient and write out your recipe poem, putting each item on a fresh line.

✳ Feel free to add suitable adjectives to your containers and your ingredients.

✳ **Hints:**
   1. Don't forget all the tiny ingredients for your recipe, such as the punctuation used in your chosen subject.

   2. Get an example of your chosen subject, and look through it, to help you find the ingredients it is made of.

 Cracking Creative Writing by David Horner © Brilliant Publications Limited. *This page may be copied by the purchasing institution only.*

The Car's the Star!

Toyota Starchaser – Tremendously Superior
Audi Whirlwind – Awesomely Wham-tastic
Hyundai Mega-Mover – Happily Massive
Vauxhall Invincible – Vehemently Incredible
Ferrari Roadscorcher – Fantastically Rapid
Suzuki Nimble – Simply Nifty
Renault Dropdeadgorgeous – Ridiculously Desirable

Extract from class-made collection

Marianne Moore was a 20th century poet. She lived mostly in New York. In the 1950s, one of the bosses of the Ford Motor Company asked her to come up with names for a new car they were building. Here are just some of her ideas:

Silver Sword, Hurricane Hirundo, Turcitonga, Mongoose Civique, Intelligent Whale, Cresta Lark, Taper Racer, Utopian Turtletop, Resilient Bullet, Turbotorc, Pastelogram, Dearborn Diamante.

Splendid, aren't they? But Ford didn't choose any of them. Instead, they called the new model the Edsel – after the son of the founder of the business, Henry Ford. It was a huge flop. The Ford Edsel is often included in lists of the 50 worst cars ever built.

Now it's your turn to name – and advertise – some cars. Be sure you read all the details below before you start writing. And have a thesaurus handy.

✱ Imagine you have been asked by several motor manufacturers to come up with names for new models. Begin by writing a list down your page of eight to ten different car manufacturers.

✱ Next, come up with a name for a new model for each of your manufacturers. Be like Marianne Moore – wacky, eye- and ear-catching, extravagant. Absolutely no Edsels!

✱ Now the manufacturers want you to write a slogan for each model. Here are their rules:
  1. Each slogan must be short and snappy. Just two words.
  2. Each two-word slogan must follow an adverb + adjective pattern, as in the examples above.
  3. Each slogan must be alliterative, again like the examples above. So, the initial letters of your two-word slogans must be the same as the initial letters of your car make and model.

✱ **Hint:** Use your thesaurus to help you find car model and slogan ideas.

✱ If cars aren't your thing, you might fancy motorbikes, bikes or trainers instead.

Stop the Clock!

Stop the Clock!

The silver hatchback sparkles in the sunshine. My wet towel dries as I wipe water all over the car's clean body. I point a hose pipe at the car. It sucks up every drop of the cold, clear water and swallows it down. With my yellow sponge I slowly remove warm, soapy water from the car and cover it in dust and dirt.

Kieran

Of course, you can't really stop the clock. However, when you write you can make anything happen. You can even make time go backwards, just like Kieran did when he un-washed the car!

And now it's your turn. Read all the details below before you start writing.

* You are going to make the ordinary extraordinary. So, to begin, choose one very ordinary, everyday activity.

* Here are some suggestions.

  At home: cleaning your teeth, making a cup of tea.
  In school: sharpening a pencil, queuing for lunch.
  Outdoors: scoring a goal, falling over and cutting a knee.

* Feel free to choose one of these – or one you have thought of yourself.

* Write down your activity, in clear, simple steps, from what you do first to what you do last. Five or six steps are quite enough. Read Kieran's piece backwards and work out what he noted down first.

* Now write the activity 'backwards', beginning with the last step and ending with the first.

* Remember, the steps are going backwards, and the action within each step must also be in reverse – like the hose pipe sucking up the water in Kieran's writing.

* Further suggestions: if reverse writing was fun, then there are lots of other topics to try. For example, a frog going back to become spawn; an oak tree reversing to become just one tiny acorn; a postman un-delivering a letter.

Cracking Creative Writing by David Horner © Brilliant Publications Limited. This page may be copied by the purchasing institution only.

Incredible Ice Creams!

TUTTI-FRUTTI STEWED TOMATO
AVOCADO BRUSSELS SPROUT
CAULIFLOWER COLA MUSTARD

Those are just three of the twenty-eight mad-cap flavours Jack Prelutsky invented for his poem, 'Bleezer's Ice Cream'.

Here are some more ice creams – genuine ones this time from around the world:

White chocolate, banana curry
Maple syrup, salted nuts, liquid nitrogen
Fresh fruits, chocolate syrup, cheddar cheese
Chopped smoked cherry, bone marrow
Butter ice cream, cooked lobster

Now it's your turn. Read all the details below before you start writing.

✳ You are going to set up your own ice cream business. The name of the business is your name + 'Ice Cream'. Write this at the top of your page. Don't forget to add apostrophe 's' after your name, as in 'BLEEZER'S ICE CREAM'.

✳ Begin by writing a short list of at least six everyday flavours you do know, each one on a new line.

✳ Now you need to add to each of these your new flavours. To get people interested in your ice creams these need to be very fresh, new, exciting – impossibly incredible – flavours.

✳ Now you are going to make your ice creams even more eye- and ear-catching than those above!

✳ To do this each of your new flavours must begin with the same letter or letters as the first, ordinary flavour. For example,

Strawberry, salmon, spaghetti
Lemon, lentil, lava
Chocolate mint chip, cheese mud chilli

Some Truly Super Supermarkets!

Some Truly Super Supermarkets!

Aldi advertises appetising alligators and awkward anchors.
Sainsbury's sells seasick seashells and slimy staircases.
Morrisons offers mean magic and monstrous moonlight.
The Co-op has concrete cake and cardboard cats.

Leon, Yusuf and Max

Now it is your turn.

First, read all the details below before you start your writing.

✳ Write the title at the top of your page.

✳ Now, think of our different supermarkets. How many can you come up with?

✳ Write the name of each one on a fresh line. Leave one or two lines between each one so you have plenty of room to write your ideas.

✳ You are going to describe just two things each supermarket sells.

✳ However, alliteration is the name of this game, so your items for sale must start with the initial letter of each of the supermarkets.

✳ Each item needs an alliterating adjective.

✳ Oh, one last thing: your chosen items must be things the actual supermarket definitely does not sell!

✳ Be as wildly imaginative as you can. Get a dictionary to help you find some incredible items and some astonishing adjectives.

***Cracking Creative Writing** by David Horner © Brilliant Publications Limited. This page may be copied by the purchasing institution only.*

Teach Yourself Venusian

Weklint, weklint, eltilt stra,
Ohw I donrew thaw uyo era!
Pu boave het drowl os ghhi,
Ekil a maddion ni het ksy.

Beth and Simon

That's an example of the language spoken on Venus. It's a translation of one of our best-known nursery rhymes, 'Twinkle, twinkle, little star'.

Scientists looking for life on Venus from millions of years ago discovered an actual example of Venusian writing buried in a cave. When they looked more closely, they realised, to their amazement, that Venusian is exactly like English – same punctuation, same grammar, same words – only the letters of each word are in a different order. This means that English words and Venusian words are anagrams of one another.

Now it's your turn to write some Venusian. Be sure you read all the details below before you start writing.

∗ Choose a short piece of English you want to translate. This can be another nursery rhyme, part or all of a poem, the opening to a novel, some scientific explanation, a bit of biography – in fact, any text you want to work on.

∗ Here are the few simple rules:

∗ Remember, the punctuation of Venusian is the same as English. Don't miss anything!

∗ Always check you have included all the letters from each English word in your translation. No spelling mistakes!

∗ If a word appears more than once, then it must be spelled exactly the same every time.

∗ If you translate a rhymed text, then see how close to a fresh rhyme you can get with your Venusian translation. For example, day and pay might become ady and apy; walking and talking could be wigklan and tigklan.

What Am I?

What Am I?

I smell money to be won.
I feel my stomach spinning and spinning.
I hear people cheering and clapping.
I see the balls dropping down into me.
I taste the winning numbers.
                    Richard

There are lots of riddles with the title, 'Who Am I?' The answer is usually an animal or an object of some sort. However, in 'What Am I?' riddles, the answer is always a machine. Can you guess Richard's? It's at the bottom of the page if you're stuck.

Now it's your turn. Be sure you read all the details below before you start writing.

✳ Your first task is to choose your machine. Any one you like: small and ordinary or huge and complicated.

✳ Now imagine you are this machine. You are alive; you can speak; and you have all five senses.

   What will your machine say it tastes, eats, drinks?
   What will it say it touches and feels?
   What will it say it sees, watches, notices?
   What will it say it breathes in and smells?
   What will it say it hears and listens to?

✳ You can write a short five-line riddle – one line for each sense. Or you might write more than one line for any one sense. So, for example, when Ian wrote his riddle, his television said:

   I feel the carpet with my feet
   And the wall with my three fingers.

✳ Above all, write clues that bring your machine vividly to life. Here's how Emma ends her telephone riddle:

   I eavesdrop on your secrets, I know all about you.

(The answer is the National Lottery draw machine.)

One Word Riddles

What Word Am I?
I have exactly eight letters
I am made out of five consonants and three vowels.
I am a noun.
The end of me is a girl's name.
You can open me up.
                    Chloe and Charlie

So, what one word is the answer? That's right – umbrella.

Now it's your turn. Be sure you read all the details below before you start writing. Have a dictionary and a thesaurus handy.

✳ In riddles like these, one word is going to describe itself and so give clues to its identity. So, first of all, choose a word that will be the answer to your riddle.

✳ Write the title, What Word Am I? and remember to write each new clue on a fresh line.

✳ You are writing as if you are the word and it is speaking for itself. This means you will be writing your riddle in the first person.

✳ Here are the bits of information you need to write down, so your word can be guessed. Just use the ones that work for your word:

  • The number of letters in your word.
  • The number of vowels and consonants in your word.
  • The part of speech – verb, noun, adjective, etc. – that your word is. You can check this by looking your word up in your dictionary. If a word can be more than one part of speech, you must say so. For example, 'play' can be both a noun and a verb.
  • Does your word have any synonyms – words meaning the same as your word? You can check this in your thesaurus. If you find one you like, begin this line, 'Another word like me is... .'
  • Does your word have any antonyms – words meaning the opposite of your word? If you know, or can find one, begin your line, 'A word that means the opposite to me is... .'
  • Does your word have any interesting features – something unusual about its spelling, repeated letters, another word inside it? If so, you can begin a line, 'One odd thing about me is... .'

✳ Finally, write a clue to your word's meaning. Nothing too obvious, nothing too vague.

Transformers

Transformers

Transform one small, sour fruit to make one large, sweet fruit.
Reorder a piece of footwear to create a long, bendy tube.
Mess up a planet to fashion two limbs.
Twist some music to get a big kiss.
Jumble a tiny boat to build a vast sea.

Rebekah and Nathan

Each line of that piece is a riddle.
Each riddle has two one-word answers.
Each of the two words will have exactly the same letters, but in a different order.
So, each word is an **anagram** of the other.

The answers to the first riddle are *lemon* and *melon*. See if you can solve the next four riddles yourself. The answers are at the bottom of the page.

Now it's your turn. Be sure you read all the details below before you start writing. You need a dictionary and a thesaurus.

✱ The first riddle starts with 'Transform'. The first word of each of the riddles that follow are synonyms for this verb. Note down any more you can think of and use your thesaurus to collect more again.

✱ The first riddle has the word 'make'. Look at the other riddles and you'll see each uses a synonym for this verb. Again, note down any more you can think of and use your thesaurus to collect more again.

✱ Now you're ready to do some transforming! To get you started, here are 10 words that have good anagrams. Work out the anagram and use any you like as well as words you think of for yourself. Stick to short, three to five letter words.

paws   top   skin   hare   rats   eat   tale   paces   ape   inch

✱ Now write your own Transformers. Use the definitions of words in your dictionary to help you compose the clues. Keep your clues clear – not too obvious, not too vague.

✱ Remember to use your Transform and make synonyms in each riddle. This means your riddles will transform words as well as letters.

Answers: shoe/hose; Mars/arms; song/snog; canoe/ocean

Colour Riddles

This red runs round us all.
This red swallows letters.
This red goes very well with cream.
   And this red says, 'Stop!'
              Danielle

Can you guess them, the four red things? The answers are at the bottom of the page, if you're stuck.

Now it's your turn. Be sure you read all the details below before you start writing.

✳ Choose a colour. Note down five or six things that are always or usually this colour. So, for example, for black, midnight is ok, but crayon is not – crayons come in all sorts of colours.

✳ From your list of items, keep four – four that are very different from one another. So, for green, not lettuce, cabbage, broccoli and sprout!

✳ Now write your four colour riddles. Each riddle must be a clue to the colour item, but don't use the name of the item itself in your clue. It's no good writing, 'This white is a snowman', if the answer is a snowman!

✳ The challenge is to write teasing clues – not too easy, not too obscure. If you're not sure, try your clues out on someone before you commit to them.

✳ Set your four riddles out like Danielle, each one on a new line, starting, 'This…', 'This…', This…', 'And this…'.

✳ Once you feel confident with your riddle-writing, try making pairs of riddles using contrasting colours – black and white, red and blue, for example. If you feel very inspired, try making a whole rainbow of riddles – four riddles for each of the seven colours.

Answers: blood, post box, strawberries, traffic light

Riddle-y-Diculous!

I am as tall as a lighthouse.
My skin is thunder cloud grey.
You can find me where hedgehogs burrow.
Pablo Picasso once owned one of me.
I can swim, but only upstream.
Never try to eat me in a sandwich.
What am I?

Maddy and Isabel

This activity comes straight from a poem by Martyn Wiley and Ian McMillan, called 'Three Riddled Riddles'. They are completely unsolvable riddles in which the poets offer a number of crazy and comical non-clues. They end each with the usual riddle question, 'What Am I?' Their answers to their three riddles are: 'I've forgotten'; 'I'm not sure'; 'I've really no idea'.

They are, then, anti-riddles full of non-clues. You never try to solve them; instead, as in the extract above by Maddy and Isabel, you just enjoy its impossibly wacky details and the way it makes gentle fun of riddle conventions.

Now it's your turn. Be sure you read all the details below before you start writing.

* There are no excuses for dull ideas here. Just be as inventive, as bizarre, as extravagant in your non-clues as you can.

* Each non-clue must sound as if it belongs in a real riddle, but don't write lots of non-clues for each riddle. It's much better to concentrate your ideas into a few lines of craziness.

* Don't forget to add your 'What Am I?' at the end of each of your anti-riddles. You can even borrow Martyn and Ian's answers, if you like, in honour of their original Riddled Riddles.

Off with Their Heads!

This is a riddle-writing game. In these riddles, the first letter of a chosen word is removed to leave a new, different word. For example, hear to ear; weight to eight. These riddles are called **Beheadments**.

The riddle always has two lines, with each line giving a clue to each word.

The first line begins *Behead* and the second line starts *to leave*. Here are two examples:

> *Behead a place for football*
> *to leave a little tickle.*
>
> > *Behead some farm animals*
> > *to leave their food.*

And the answers are: pitch and itch; goats and oats.

Now it's your turn. Be sure you read all the details below before you start writing.

✳   Have a dictionary handy. You can use it to hunt suitable words – and use the definitions to help you design your clues.

✳   **Hint 1:** Don't make your clues too easy or too difficult. Too easy and there's no fun for your readers. Too hard and they'll just give up.

✳   **Hint 2:** If you can have a link between your two clues – as in the second example above – that would look very clever indeed!

✳   **Hint 3:** Another clever trick is to find words which can be beheaded more than once. For example, crash to rash to ash; space to pace to ace. Here is a final example for you to work out the three words:

> *Behead someone who doesn't play fair*
> *to leave strong warmth.*
>
> *Behead the warmth*
> *to leave what we do with food.*

Answer: cheat to heat; heat to eat.

Chop Off Their Tails!

This is a riddle-writing idea. It's a game in which letters are removed from words, but whereas in Beheadments, words lost their first letter, here it is the last letter of a word that gets removed each time to leave a new, different word. For example, sight to sigh; puffing to puffin. These riddles are called **Curtailments**. The word 'curtail' means to cut short.

The riddle always has two lines, with each line giving a clue to each word.

The first line begins *Curtail* and the second line starts *to leave*. Here are two examples:

> *Curtail a lot of people*
> *to leave one black bird.*
>
> *Curtail the hair on dad's face,*
> *to leave a huge and hairy creature.*

And the answers are: crowd and crow; beard and bear.

Now it's your turn. Be sure you read all the details below before you start writing.

✳ Have a dictionary handy. You can use it to hunt suitable words – and use the definitions to help you design your clues.

✳ **Hint 1:** Don't make your clues too easy or too difficult. If they're too easy, there's no fun for your readers. If they're too hard, they'll just give up.

✳ **Hint 2:** Sometimes you might find a word that works well if you remove more than one letter from the end – for example, hum/an, arm/our. In these cases, simply begin your Curtailment riddle, Curtail… twice; Curtail… three times.

✳ **Hint 3:** If you can have a link between your two clues – as in the second example above – that would look very clever indeed!

✳ **Hint 4:** You might think of or find a word that you can curtail – and also behead. Here, to finish, is an example for you to work out the four words.

> *Curtail your backbone*
> *to leave what roundabouts do.*
>
> *Behead what roundabouts do*
> *to leave something small, shiny and sharp.*
>
> *Behead the small, shiny, sharp thing*
> *to leave the opposite of out.*

Answers: spine and spin; spin and pin; pin and in.

 Cracking Creative Writing by David Horner © Brilliant Publications Limited. This page may be copied by the purchasing institution only.

Although...

> *Although I have four legs, I'm not a table.*
> *Although I have a wet nose, I'm not a dog.*
> *Although I am large, I'm not an elephant.*
> *Although I live on a farm, I'm not a horse.*
> *Although I give you milk, I'm not a goat.*
>
> *Freya*

Can you guess Freya's riddle? If not, the answer is at the end of the page.

Now it's your turn. Read all the details below before you start writing.

✳ Choose an animal that will be the answer to your riddle. Note down four to six features of this animal. These will give you the four to six lines of your riddle.

✳ Take each feature in turn and write one line of your riddle. Write these lines in any order you like. Begin the line, 'Although I' and add the feature. Complete the line with another animal or thing that also has this feature but is not the correct answer.

✳ Now write a last draft of your riddle, putting your lines into a final order. Take care here, because someone guessing your riddle is building a mental picture, one detail at a time. So, for example, line 3 of Freya's riddle couldn't be, 'Although I am large, I'm not a whale,' because we already know from line 1 that her creature has four legs.

✳ Here's an old riddle using this form:

> *Though not a cow, I have horns.*
> *Though not an ass, I carry a pack-saddle.*
> *And wherever I go, I leave silver behind me.*

The answer to Freya's riddle is a cow. The answer to the bottom riddle is a snail.

The Song of the Syllables

A cool cat.
A daft dog.
A slow snail.

A gentle giraffe.
A silent spider.
A ticklish tiger.

An eccentric elephant.
Lewis

Now it is your turn.

First, read all the details below before you start your writing.

✳ Now, I'm sure you can already see how this writing game might go!

✳ For each verse of your list poem you need some animals.

✳ For verse one, you need one-syllable animals; and each animal needs a one-syllable alliterating adjective.

✳ For verse two, you need two-syllable animals, each with a two-syllable alliterating adjective.

✳ How far can you go? There are lots of animals with four syllables in their names!

✳ Be sure you check the syllable-count in all the words you choose. Say each word clearly to yourself and just count the beats. Every beat is a syllable. Here's an example using names:

Ann (1 beat), Annie (Ann – ie = 2 beats), Annika (An – ik – a = 3 beats).

✳ If it helps, use the names of friends in the class to practise checking beats and syllables.

✳ A thesaurus will help your animal hunting. A dictionary will help you track down some good adjectives.

✳ As well as animals, you can try the same idea using foods, vehicles, place names, football teams. And maybe you can think of more?

Scrambled Senses – or the Strange World of Synaesthesia!

Synaesthesia is when...

Red roses taste like electric guitars.
Spaghetti bolognese looks like the wind on your face.
My cat's fur smells of lightning.
New shoes sound like pale blue.
A whistle tastes like my cat's tongue.

A group-made poem

What if you could smell a sound? Or taste a colour? Or listen to a flavour as in that poem you've just read?

There's a proper name for this mixing of the five senses: it's **synaesthesia**. You say it like this: sy-ness-these-ia.

Some people have this ability – and you are going to explain and define the phenomenon in what you write.

Read all the details below before you start writing.

✳ Begin with some notes. First, write down each of your five senses one under the other.

✳ Beside each sense write two or three things you experience with it. So for smell, you might have sweaty socks, cut grass or mum's perfume. Let's call these sense objects.

✳ Get a clean sheet of paper and fold it in half lengthways.

✳ At the top of your page write, 'Synaesthesia is when…'

✳ Down the middle of your folded paper now write the five sensing verbs: looks like; sounds like; tastes like; feels like; smells like.

✳ Using your notes made earlier and to the left of each sense verb write any one sense object that doesn't belong with the verb.

✳ Use your list again and now to the right of the verb, add a sense object – that doesn't fit the first sense object OR the verb.

✳ Each line should therefore include three different senses. Look back at any of the lines in the poem at the top to help you.

I'd Rather...

I'd rather be a hammer than a nail.
I'd rather be a shark than a whale.

I'd rather be cool than hot,
I'd rather be a bed than a cot.

I'd rather be a hawk than a hen.
I'd rather be twenty than ten.

I'd rather be a tree than a log.
I'd much rather run than jog.

Adrian

This idea comes from a line of the song 'El Cóndor Pasa' (If I Could) by the singer/songwriter Paul Simon.

Now it's your turn.

Read all the details below before you start writing.

✳ Adrian started by borrowing Paul Simon's opening line and you can do the same, if you like.

✳ Next, you need a rather/than line that rhymes with nail.

✳ The rhyme word can be:
    a noun, as in Adrian's whale, so tail, jail, for example;
    an adjective – pale, stale;
    a verb – fail, sail.

✳ And, of course you need an 'opposite' to your rhyme word; so, for example, head/tail; succeed/fail; bright/pale.

✳ Write your rhyme line underneath the first line and when you have finished your first two lines, you have a rhyming couplet. Now see how many more couplets you can make.

✳ Each time you start a new couplet, you can have any words and ideas you like. Only the second line has to rhyme.

✳ **Hint:** If you get stuck for a rhyme, just go through the alphabet in your head adding the rhyme-sound to see what real rhyming words come up for you to choose from. And if you have a rhyming dictionary – use it!

Odd One In

> A window cleaner carries his ladder on his shoulder on a warm day.
> A nurse talks quietly to a very old man.
> A police lady writes something in her notebook.
> A silver party balloon finally lands in a field in Holland.
> A shop assistant sells a pair of shiny new shoes.
> A TV repair man knocks on a door.
>
> *Joshua*

Now it's your turn…

First, read all the details below before you start your writing.

✳ Begin by writing a short list of things, animals or people that go together. For example, some kinds of weather, half a dozen items for sale in a supermarket, things you would find at the seaside.

✳ Now write down one more item that doesn't belong to your list, something or someone that's different, that doesn't fit in with the rest; an item that's odd.

✳ Now write to develop your items, by adding details to bring each one to life for a reader. Put each item on a new line.

✳ Above all, think very hard about just where you will place your odd item in the final list. Where does it make its best contrast with everything else?

A Sound Poem

M
Mo
Mov
Move
Moving

S
St
Sto
Stop
Stopp
Stoppe
Stopped

Simone

First of all, read Simone's two-word sound-poem to yourself. Read slowly, enjoying the sounds of each line before you reach the final word. You'll also see how the growing lines build to create the meanings of the two verbs.

Now it's your turn. Be sure you read all the details below before you start writing. You need a thesaurus as well as your writing materials.

✳ You need just two verbs: two verbs with opposite meanings – **antonyms**. Here are some examples. Choose from these or antonyms you have thought of:

> *come / go   appear / vanish   grow / shrink   arrive / depart   rise / fall*

✳ Next, look each verb up in your thesaurus, where you'll find synonyms for your verbs. Make a final choice of the two verbs you want to use.

✳ Now write each verb down, either adding one letter at a time as Simone did, or you might prefer to remove a letter each time, so that, for example, vanished *does* vanish and ends with just a v.

✳ **Hint**: Take care with your spelling! Notice in Simone's poem how she had to drop the e from move to make moving; and she had to double the p in stop to make stopped.

✳ Be sure to read your sound-poem out loud to yourself and others.

There IS Such a Word as Can't

Here are five things I can't do when I'm tidying my room:
I can't see granny's caravan in Talacre.
I can't taste the pizza toppings in my favourite restaurant.
I can't hear One Direction live on stage.
I can't smell the popcorn as the film is about to start.
I can't feel all the cool sand between my toes.
However, I can daydream of walking through my wardrobe to meet Hermione Granger.

Olivia

Having to do everyday jobs is, well, a chore. And a bore. One way we get through these jobs is to switch off while we do them and go into a world of our own. We start to daydream, in other words. Exactly what Olivia does.

Now it's your turn. Be sure you read all the details below before you start writing.

✳ To begin, choose any routine job you don't like doing – but you have to do it! Now write an opening line in the style of the poem above. It looks smart if you end this line with a colon; it tells the reader a list is coming.

✳ This list will be five favourite things you can't do while you're toiling away. One thing for each of your five senses. So: smell, taste, touch, hearing, sight.

✳ Make every 'can't' in your list very different. This will emphasise how trapped you are by your chore, by detailing the many things you could be doing instead.

✳ Start the final line with the word 'However'. It at once signals a change is coming, an escape, even if only in your imagination.

✳ Finish this line by writing how you will make your getaway and just what your great daydream is. Be as fantastical and extravagant as you like here – after all, you are only dreaming!

Fourteen Questions to an Alien

Alien, alien, where in space do you live?
Why are you so thin and bony?
Has your skin always been so bright green?
Are you cold like that? Do you ever wear clothes?
Your head is so big and bald. How brainy are you?
Why haven't you got ears or a nose?
Can you speak English?
Your eyes are huge. Can you see through things? Round corners? Into the future?
Are your fingers and toes sticky? Can you climb walls?
You look so serious. Are you happy?

Finn

One of the most famous English poems is 'The Tyger' by William Blake. He published it in 1794. It's very likely Blake never saw a real, live tiger. So, he must have stood and stared at a picture and got lost in amazement at such a strange and scary creature.

In the poem, Blake sees the tiger as a fire, 'burning bright'. All he can do is ask it questions: who would dare to make such a fearful creature as you? Who could be skilful enough to twist the sinews of [your] heart and bring you to life? He asks 14 questions in all.

The tiger keeps its distance and mystery by not answering any of Blake's questions.

Now it's your turn. Be sure you read all the details below before you start writing.

✳ As well as your writing materials, you need a picture of an alien, either in a book, a comic or on a screen.

✳ To Blake in the 18th century, a tiger was an alien creature – remote, strange, unknowable. You are following in his poetic footsteps, so look hard and often at your 21st century alien and start asking it your own questions.

✳ Your reader has probably never seen your alien image. Your task is to bring the alien to life through your questions, so a reader can imagine it in all its far-off otherness.

✳ Remember, your target is 14 questions, in memory of William Blake and his Tyger.

 Cracking Creative Writing by David Horner © Brilliant Publications Limited. *This page may be copied by the purchasing institution only.*

Meet the Two of Me

Sometimes I'm every episode of Dr Who,
Occasionally I can be the weather forecast.
One day I'm a newly unwrapped Nike tee shirt.
The next day I'm all my school uniform.
Generally, I'm a silver Aston Martin DB 5,
but at times I become a rusty yellow banger with a flat battery.

Greg

We are individuals, true, but that doesn't mean we are always exactly the same. We all show different parts of ourselves and our personalities, depending on where we are and who we are with. This writing idea seeks to recognise this variety within each of us.

Now it's your turn. Be sure you read all the details below before you start writing.

✻ Start by writing two lists: one of likes and one of dislikes for six to eight different things. For example: food tastes, TV programmes, times of day, weathers, books, music, smells, drinks, clothes, film characters, places. Feel free to use any of these, plus ideas of your own.

✻ Make sure, for each idea you do choose, you write down a liked and a disliked item.

✻ You're ready to start creating your lines now. Pairs of lines, in fact. For each pair, you need two phrases to introduce them. Look back at ones Greg used, *Sometimes / Occasionally*, etc. Here are some more:

Usually / but at times
Most days / from time to time
Typically / but every now and then
As a rule / but now and again
By and large / once in a while
More often than not / but just once in a blue moon

✻ Write your introductions and follow each with phrases such as 'I am', 'I can become', 'I might be', 'I change into'.

✻ Finally, you can now complete each pair of lines by adding two matched items from your collection.

The Best Poem in the World...Ever!

This poem can tell the time without a watch.
It has butterfly wings.
The poem was once red, green and blue.
Long ago it passed an exam.
The poem dreams about being in Swan Lake.
One day this poem will touch the sky.

Siad and Helen

Now it is your turn.

First, read all the details below before you start your writing.

✳ Write the title at the top of your paper. Don't forget the ellipsis!

✳ You really have to think big and bold here! If this is the best poem ever, it must look the part; it must act the part.

✳ Here are some suggestions for lines to get you started. Use any of these you want – plus some ideas of your own.

What marvellous things can your poem do?
What does it look like?
Does it have a favourite food and drink?
What does it like doing best of all?
What does it want to do?
Where was it born?
What does it dream about?
Where did you find it?
Did someone own it before you?
What will become of it in the future?

✳ Aim for at least six lines of amazingness!

The Four Elements

> Dolphins leap through the flames of the sun.
> In the deep Indian Ocean hedgehogs are swimming.
> A huge gorilla is flying slowly over Mount Everest.
> On the only cloud in the sky an octopus sits.
> *Megan*

The four elements are fire, water, earth and air. It was an ancient Greek and Indian belief that everything was made from them. Look back and you'll find examples of all four elements in Megan's verse.

Now it's your turn. Read all the details below before you start writing.

✳ Each line of Megan's verse is a **koan**. Koans come from Buddhist beliefs in China and Japan. They are puzzles or riddles – to which there are no answers. Not nonsense, exactly, but rather things to exercise our brains and develop our imaginations. And every one of us can surely imagine those creatures in those unusual settings.

✳ Begin your writing with some quick notes.

✳ Jot down each element, and after each one, add an animal – one that definitely doesn't belong there.

✳ Now start creating each koan. Don't just use the basic name of each element, but rather think of a particular example to represent each element. Megan had the sun for her fire and Mount Everest for her earth.

✳ To give your writing variety, use both the present (flies) and the progressive (are swimming) forms of your verbs.

✳ Also, vary your sentence structures by having the animal first and the element second in two of your lines and the element first and the animal second in the other two.

✳ If you have time, write a second four-line verse, with fresh animals and different examples of each element.

Impossible Demands

> ***Fetch me*** a velociraptor's skull in a silver teapot.
> ***I must have*** the north wind on a glass saucer.
> ***I am ordering*** the roar of twelve African lions in a wizard's hat.
> ***I want*** the whole of Antarctica in a straw basket.
> ***Go and get me*** a black storm cloud on a golden dinner plate.
> ***Bring me*** the sunset in a cup.
>
> *Harriet*

Fictional queens and kings are always making demands. Remember Old King Cole calling for his pipe, his bowl and his fiddlers three? Or King Lear, tragically ordering the love and obedience of his three daughters? Most demanding of all perhaps was Lewis Carroll's waspish Queen of Hearts, ruling her Wonderland through fear, yelling for a fresh beheading about once a minute.

Now it's your turn. Be sure you read all the details below before you start writing. Have a thesaurus handy.

✳ In this activity, you simply have to see yourself as a queen or a king – or ruler of the world, if you like!

✳ And because you are now all-powerful, you are going to test your staff and servants by making some really impossible demands. Not wicked, cruel or harmful; just…impossible.

✳ Look back to Harriet's last line: 'Bring me the sunset in a cup'. She was given this line as a model to work from. Instead of starting with it, she used it to be her ending. It was actually written by Emily Dickinson, an American poet, who was not at all bossy and queen-like. She lived almost her whole life, very privately and quietly, in just one house.

✳ Here are the elements you need for each line:

✳ Begin by signalling the order. You can use some of Harriet's openings: 'Fetch me', 'I must have', etc. and use your thesaurus to find more.

✳ Next, write the thing you are demanding: things from the natural world, remote parts of the earth, the weather, outer space. Remember, no animals must be injured in the writing of your poem!

✳ Finally, write how you would like it served to you. Add details here to make it sound grand and impressive. This all helps the simple last line work well as a contrast.

 Cracking Creative Writing by David Horner © Brilliant Publications Limited. This page may be copied by the purchasing institution only.

Different Things to Different People

> ### Different Things to Different People
>
> *To my dad I'm a getter of drinks.*
> **To my mum I'm a too long sleeper in bed.**
> *To my sister I'm a punchbag.*
> **To my gran I'm a total genius.**
> *To my dog I'm a taker for walks and a poo bagger.*
> **To my bedroom I'm a champion mess maker.**
> *To my mates I'm the quickest Rubik's cube doer.*
>
> Gavin

It seems everyone who knows us sees us slightly – sometimes very – differently.

And now it's your turn. Be sure you read all the details below before you start writing.

✱ Note down the family members, friends, neighbours, teachers, pets, places you know and who know you.

✱ Now think about each of these and ask yourself how they see you. If asked, what one thing would they say about you? Note your thoughts beside each person, pet, place, etc.

✱ Write the title at the top of your page.

✱ In any order you like, work through your list, beginning each on a new line, 'To my…I'm'.

✱ Complete each line with your idea of how they see you.

✱ **Hint 1:** As in Gavin's poem a very good way of making some of your lines is to use what's called a kenning.

✱ A **kenning** is a verb that gets made into a noun. So, for example, in Gavin's poem, he gets (verb) drinks for his dad; he sleeps (verb) over-long; he takes (verb) his dog for walks. As nouns these become getter, sleeper, taker. Usually putting '-er' on the end of the basic verb will do the job for you.

✱ **Hint 2:** To finish your poem, try starting a line, 'And to myself I'm...'

The Most Important Date in the History of the Universe!

The Most Important Date in the History of the Universe!

On the day that I was born,
seven rainbows appeared in the sky,
The Rolling Stones played in the hospital grounds,
tigers and zebras swapped stripes,
aliens on Pluto danced the Hokey-Cokey
and J K Rowling wrote a special story just for me.

Niamh (extract)

Now it's your turn. Be sure you read all the details below before you start writing.

∗ The day you were born has to be – for you – the most important date ever. Unfortunately, though you were there, you don't remember a thing about it. This means you are free to celebrate by making the whole day up – as madly, as improbably, as imaginatively as you can!

∗ Begin with a title: the date of your birth. If you know which day of the week it was, you can include that too.

∗ Underneath, write that opening line, 'On the day that I was born,'.

∗ Now make up as many wondrous events as you can to celebrate your arrival. The only rule is: nothing dull and everyday. Each new line must add to the energy and excitement of the event.

∗ Here are some ideas to help you get started:

What about a historical figure coming to visit?
Maybe a fictional character turns up too?
Describe the weather on the day.
Maybe some of the world's wild animals join in the celebration.
In some far-off city or country, they celebrate. How?
There might be wild goings-on in outer space.
What marvellous music and performers welcome you?

∗ Feel free to use any or all of these ideas plus ones of your own.

∗ Feel free also to repeat the opening line as often as you like, to remind your readers just why there is all this excitement.

∗ If you wish, end your celebration poem by naming your very favourite writer and what they wrote as your unique birthday piece.

Well Done, Me!

Well Done, Me!

Today I am congratulating myself because:
• I haven't fallen out with anyone yet;
• I ate almost all my breakfast;
• I cleaned my teeth really well;
• I remembered my kit for PE;
• I sang all the words of my favourite song to myself;
• I put my hand up more than once in class;
• I've lent my rubber to three people;
• I've proved that I can now use colons, semicolons and bullet points correctly!

Rachael

We congratulate people and give them awards all the time – but usually for big and important achievements: medals in the Olympics, cups in football, certificates for passing examinations, for example.

But every day we all of us achieve small, ordinary things, and usually nobody knows about them but us. So now is your chance to write and recognise any or all of your everyday successes.

Be sure you read all the details below before you start writing.

✳ Write the title at the top of your paper.

✳ Write a line to introduce your list of achievements. You can borrow Rachael's or make one like it of your own.

✳ Now write your list of achievements. You can include things you've done in the past hour, in the day so far, it's up to you. Nothing you've done recently is too small or trivial to be included!

✳ Finally, in case you are wondering about Rachael's last line:

• A colon is used to introduce a list or an explanation.
• One use of a semicolon is to divide items in a list, where each item is quite long.
• Bullet points introduce items in a list, instead of numbers.

✳ So, she was quite right to congratulate herself. And you can do the same if you wish!

Excuses, Excuses!

Why, today, I will not fly to the Moon

It's raining, and I don't want my rocket to get wet.
I've been there so many times already.
I have to revise for a history test.
I've suddenly become scared of heights.
The Man in the Moon has gone on holiday,
and there'll be nobody there to play with.
Dad wants me to tidy my room,
so I think, instead, I'll become invisible.

Carl

We all make excuses, some to get to do something – stay up late, have new trainers; and others to get out of doing something – a chore, visiting grandad.

And we need to be good at making excuses! It's an arguing skill we need to practise from an early age.

Now it's your turn. Be sure you read all the details below before you start writing.

∗ Think of some power, ability or skill – one you don't have, but one you'd very much like to have. The more amazing and impossible, the better. For example,

You are Superman or Wonder Woman.
You can swim the Atlantic.
You can spell any English word correctly.
You can grow 10 feet tall.

∗ And, just like Carl, you have this power – but today you just don't feel like using it.

∗ When you've chosen your power, write your title: 'Why, today, I will not' and add your power.

∗ Now write your excuses – as many different ones as you can think of. You can always cross out ones you don't think are good enough later. This way, you are really practising your excuse-making skills!

∗ **Hint:** Maybe finish your great excuses poem, like Carl, by introducing a new, different ability you do want to show off.

 Cracking Creative Writing by David Horner © Brilliant Publications Limited. *This page may be copied by the purchasing institution only.*

And the Award Goes to...

> *High-fives to my dad for shaving his beard off. Give a big hand to my Brownie Sixer, Ashlee, for all the fun. A pat on the back for Mrs Hershfield for teaching me fractions. Hang out the flags for my mum for taking me to gymnastics. Three cheers for Roald Dahl for all of his stories. And the Award goes to – my dog Cassie for keeping my feet warm!*
>
> *Nadine*

We have lots of ways of congratulating and celebrating people. You've just read the ones Nadine begins her sentences with. Here are a few more:

Raise a cheer for…
Roll out the red carpet for…
Hand out bouquets to…
Blow the trumpets for…

And you might even think of more for yourself or find more in a thesaurus.

Now it's your turn. Be sure you read all the details below before you start writing.

✳ First, before you write the actual details of your Awards piece, make a list of the family members, friends, people who are important to you, the pets you are going to include. As many as you like. These are your nominees. From these nominees, pick out the one who will get the Award – and therefore feature in your final line, as Nadine does.

✳ Now compose your Awards nominations, one by one. You can write your award sentences in a list form – one below the other – if you wish.

✳ Start each nomination with one of those celebration phrases, taking care not to repeat any.

✳ Next write whoever is being nominated.

✳ Finish the nomination by saying why you are nominating them.

✳ Begin your last sentence, 'And the Award goes to…'. And, of course, say why.

Big Yourself Up!

> *Saskia H – you are the greatest.*
> *You are fabulous and excellent.*
> *You finish first and always get full marks in every school test.*
> *Your brother and older sister think you are wonderful.*
> *You will be the greatest ballet dancer ever.*
> *You will be the first woman to walk on Mars.*
> *The rain stops when you say so.*
> *You are the greatest, Saskia H.*

Now it's your turn. Be sure you read all the details below before you start writing.

✳ There's no room here for you to be shy and modest. No putting yourself down, no under-valuing yourself. Make the most of yourself – and more. Praise yourself as you have never done before!

✳ As Saskia did, begin by writing your name; add a dash and write, *you are the greatest*.

✳ Write *You are* and then at least two adjectives about yourself. Very flattering ones!

✳ Now write some lines about how your friends, family, teachers and other adults in your life rate you. Don't forget, they all agree: you are the greatest.

✳ Next, write some lines about your skills, talents and achievements – including ones you've told no one about before.

✳ Next, write some very impressive ambitions for the future.

✳ Write at least one line in which the natural or the supernatural world recognises your wonderfulness.

✳ You can end if you wish, like Saskia, by echoing your opening line.

✳ Think and write quickly, aiming for up to ten lines in all. If you have time, write a second draft, putting your lines into a different order, one that you prefer.

BIG Fibs

> Sweets taste disgusting.
> My brother is a Martian.
> Elephants are the smallest creatures on earth.
> Buckingham Palace has disappeared.
> Laura only wears green clothes.
> My mum was once in a pop band.
> *Tamsin, Becky and Alex*

Now it is your turn.

First, read all the details below before you start your writing.

✱ Think of people and things to write fibs about. The wilder your ideas, the better. Remember, you are writing BIG fibs!

✱ Aim for lots of variety, both in what you write about and the fib you tell.

✱ Think and write quickly; aim for between eight and ten subjects in all.

✱ You could set yourself a time limit and see how many you can come up with in this time.

✱ Write each BIG fib on a new line.

✱ Make a final draft of your fibs, writing them in the order in which you like them – from your least favourite down to your most favourite.

✱ Finally, a few more ideas for you to fib about…a tv programme; where you live; a supermarket; an animal; your pencil.

Cracking Creative Writing by David Horner © Brilliant Publications Limited. *This page may be copied by the purchasing institution only.*

Weather Warnings

> **Don't take off**
> **with a Zombie**
> **on a barge**
> **in the heavy rain.**
> *Kenneth Koch*

Who knows what those four short lines mean! But it's probably good advice – if you ever meet a Zombie.

And now it's your turn. Have a dictionary handy.

Read all the details below before you start your writing.

✳ **Line 1:** Begin with 'Don't' or a synonym such as 'Never' or 'Be sure not to'. Open your dictionary at any page and find a verb you like to finish line 1.

✳ **Line 2:** Begin with 'with a' or a synonym such as 'near to a' or 'alongside a'. Finish the line with any alien or extinct creature, such as a diplodocus or hobgoblin. Don't forget the capital letter for your creature because it is a proper noun.

✳ **Line 3:** Begin 'on a' or with any other preposition, such as 'beside', 'in', 'under', 'close to'. Open your dictionary at any page and find a noun you like to finish line 3.

✳ **Line 4:** Begin with 'in the' and then open your dictionary at any page. Find an adjective you like and write it down. Finish the line with any weather – but not rain!

✳ Repeat these activities to make as many more four-line weird weather warnings as you like.

 Cracking Creative Writing by David Horner © Brilliant Publications Limited. This page may be copied by the purchasing institution only.

Thirteen Things

Thirteen Bad Things To Do With Your Homework

Use it as a coffee mug mat.
Send it to the moon and back and tell your teacher it's not coming home for at least 2 years.
Scrunch it up to play footie with your mates.
Sail it down the river and out into the sea.
If your mum finds it, tell her it's last year's Maths piece.
Leave it on the garden path till it rains.

Graeme (extract)

In 1917, the American poet Wallace Stevens published 'Thirteen Ways of Looking at a Blackbird'. Ever since, it seems, poets have been borrowing and adapting the idea. Sixty years later, for example, the Scottish poet George MacBeth wrote 'Fourteen Ways of Touching the Peter' about his cat and the different ways it liked human contact.

Now it's your turn. Be sure you read all the details below before you start writing.

✻ Poets using Wallace Stevens' original idea always choose a particular subject. Then, in single lines or short verses, they look at their subject in a number of different ways or describe different ways of using it.

✻ So, first of all, choose your subject. It can be anything at all, from the remote and extraordinary (an iceberg, Saturn, a dream) to the everyday and very ordinary (a ruler, a pizza, a shoe).

✻ Now, either look at – or imagine – your subject and start to note down all the things you could do with it. Be as inventive, impossible, fantastical as you can. Let your imagination run free and wild! You want your readers to be entertained and excited by your ideas.

✻ When you have all the ideas you can think of, write a title such as...

Seven Ways of Using…
Ten Ways of Looking at…
Eight Things to Do With…

...and write your ideas underneath, each on a fresh line.

✻ Well done, if you do get to thirteen things. You're a member of a very exclusive club.

The Things I Did Not Do

> *This Christmas I did not*
> *fly through the sky on Rudolf's back,*
> *I never opened a present as big as a hotel,*
> *I did not meet Santa Claus in our kitchen,*
> *I did not build a snowman with a carrot for a nose,*
> *I did not find an iPhone in my cracker,*
> *and I did not eat any sprouts.*
>
> Jamie and Petra

Now it's your turn.

Read all the details below before you start your writing.

* Choose one of these three subjects: Christmas; holidays; birthday.

* These can be really dull subjects to write about – describing what you did at Christmas, where you went on your holiday, what you got on your birthday. And they can make your writing very dull too.

* But if you write about what you did not do, where you did not go, what you did not get – well, let your imagination run wild!

* Now you've chosen your subject, begin your writing 'This Christmas I did not' or 'On my holidays I did not' or 'On my birthday I did not'.

* Now think of five or six things you did not do or get or go to. Aim for lots of variety in the things you choose – extraordinary things, crazy things, impossible things – and add details to them, to bring each one fully to life, as in the poem at the top.

* Write each idea on a new line, beginning each *I did not*. This helps create the poem's overall mood.

* Until the very last line, end each line with a comma. This keeps the poem good and pacey.

* **Hint:** Keep your best *did not* until the last line, to end your poem with a flourish.

Cracking Creative Writing by David Horner © Brilliant Publications Limited. *This page may be copied by the purchasing institution only.*

A Personal Paint Box

My red is strawberries and tomato sauce.
My white is snow and ice cream.
My pink is lipstick and candy floss.
My yellow is custard and the sun.
My black is the middle of my eye and the night time.
And my gold is my trophies and pound coins in my pocket.
Laura

Now it is your turn.

First, read all the details below before you start your writing.

✳ Imagine you have a paint box. A personal one, full not just with colours, but with things that are each colour; things you like; things you have chosen.

✳ Each line of your poem must feature a different colour. You can do as many lines and colours as you like.

✳ Begin each of your lines with 'My' and then write the colour.

✳ Think of two things that are this colour to complete each line.

✳ Work hard to make your two chosen things different from one another. This helps bring each colour to life and creates real interest for a reader.

Happy Birthday, Moon!

I will give you
a red hat to keep your bald head warm in space,
some yellow bananas for your midnight snacks
and
a green traffic light so astronauts can land safely on you.
I will give you
a pair of pink socks to dance in at your party,
some silver sunglasses so the sun can't blind you
and
a grey concrete bridge for you to walk down to earth.
Craig

Now it's your turn. Be sure you read all the details below before you start writing.

✳ The Moon is an empty, colourless place. It must look down on our earth and feel very envious.

✳ Well, imagine this: you have decided it's time to cheer the Moon up a bit. It's the Moon's birthday soon and you are going to give the Moon some presents – lots of different presents and every one of them a different colour.

✳ Obviously, the Moon can't understand what all our earth stuff is for, so you will have to tell it.

✳ You are giving birthday presents, so make each one sound enjoyable and interesting. Craig didn't just write, 'a red hat to wear' or 'some yellow bananas to eat'. He made each present sound exciting, something the moon would love to get – and you must do the same.

✳ You can write the introductory phrase, 'I will give you', as often as you like.

✳ Put each present on a new line. And remember, each line must include:
  • A fresh colour
  • The present
  • How the moon can use and enjoy the present.

✳ Look back and see how Craig ended each of his three-line verses with the word 'and'. If you do the same, it just makes that final line a bit more of a climax. And it shows you know how to write and finish a list!

 Cracking Creative Writing by David Horner © Brilliant Publications Limited. *This page may be copied by the purchasing institution only.*

Absolutely Adverbs

> ### Absolutely Adverbs
>
> *A arrives angrily.*
> *B behaves badly.*
> *C crumbles crazily.*
> *D dances dizzily.*
> *Extract from group piece*

When an adverb is added to a verb, it adds something extra to the verb. So, 'Grandad snores' tells us something, but 'Grandad snores softly,' or, 'Grandad snores stupendously,' tells us a little bit more.

Now it's your turn. You need a dictionary.

Read all the details below before you start writing.

✳ You are going to write an alphabet piece. Every time you write a letter of the alphabet, open your dictionary to that letter.

✳ Look through the pages covering the letter and find a verb you like. Look for the letter '*v*' after the word to check it is a verb.

✳ Write your verb next to the letter of the alphabet, adding 's' to the end of the verb.

✳ Now open your dictionary again at words starting with the same letter as the verb and find an adjective you like. Look for the letters '*adj*' after the word to check it is an adjective.

✳ Write your chosen adjective after the verb, adding '-ly' to make it into an adverb.

✳ **Hint:** When you reach X, don't panic! Look through X, of course, but also around 'ex' to find your verb and adverb.

Cracking Creative Writing by David Horner © Brilliant Publications Limited. *This page may be copied by the purchasing institution only.*

Conjunctions Rule, OK?

> *and I stood*
> *and I waited*
> *and I ran*
> *and I chased*
> *and I panted*
> *and I ran out of breath*
> *and I came second.*
> *Eddie*

✻ Conjunctions – like 'and' – link words or phrases together. Normally, when we write a list, we separate items with commas and only have 'and' before the last item.

✻ However, as in Eddie's piece, repeating the conjunction can add to the dramatic effect of the writing. We feel the effort he put in – and at the end, we're almost breathless with him!

✻ Here is a group-made piece, using the conjunction 'but':

> *I have homework*
> *but it's too hard*
> *but mum's watching me*
> *but it's boring*
> *but I want to play out*
> *but it'll be all wrong*
> *but my mates are calling round*
> *but there's something good on telly*
> *but I have homework.*

✻ Here are some more conjunctions:

> *although   if   because   now   before   or*

✻ Choose any one conjunction and to begin, write one sentence with the conjunction in the middle. For example: 'I like giraffes because…' or 'It's bed time although…' or 'I can watch Match of the Day if…'.

✻ Now write as many endings to your sentence as you can think of. One under the other.

✻ Finally, try putting your opening phrase at the very end – to keep the reader in suspense.

✻ Repeating conjunctions for dramatic effect, when they aren't strictly necessary, has a strange name: **polysyndeton.**

 Cracking Creative Writing by David Horner © Brilliant Publications Limited. *This page may be copied by the purchasing institution only.*

A Preposition Poem

Outside my head a lesson is going on.
Below my head is a neck twisting to see out the window.
Above my head is lots and lots of wild hair.
Beside my head and me is my best friend, Beth.
Inside my head is a story that wants to escape.

Rhiannon

Now it's your turn.

First, read all the details below before you start your writing.

✳ Prepositions are those useful, tiny words that often tell you where something is happening.

✳ The best example is at the panto. If there's a threat to a character, we all help by shouting out, 'It's behind you!'

✳ Begin by choosing something that interests you, that you want to focus on. It can be almost anything at all.

✳ It can be:
  • an object. For example, a box, a door, a boat.
  • an animal. For example, a whale, an eagle, an elephant.
  • a person. For example, someone famous, someone you know well, someone doing their job.
  • a place. For example, a desert, a forest, where you are right now!

✳ You choose, then think all around whatever you have chosen and write a line for each 'position', beginning each line with a fresh preposition.

✳ Here are some prepositions to help you: above, below, next to, under, around, inside, outside, over, on, close to, in front of, beside, behind, near. How many can you use?

Synonyms and Antonyms

> **The story is unhappy, sad, melancholy.**
> It is tear-jerking, miserable, sorrowful,
> **tragic.**
>
> **But the ending is smiling.**
> It is merry, delighted, joyful, sunny, optimistic,
> **happy as a pig in muck.**
> *William*

Just to remind you: **synonyms** are words that mean the same; for example, warm, hot, sizzling. **Antonyms** are words with opposite meanings; for example, hot and cold.

But English isn't as simple as that. Hot is much hotter than warm and sizzling is hotter again. Cold is colder than cool – and freezing is even colder!

So, a better definition is to say synonyms are words with similar meanings.

Now it's your turn. Be sure you read all the details below before you start writing.

✳ First, choose one of these pairs of adjective antonyms:

   hot/cold   small/big   dark/bright   slow/quick   neat/messy   noisy/quiet   bad/good

✳ Next, decide on a theme for your writing; for example:

   hot day/cold drink   dark night/bright moon   slow tortoise/quick hare

   bad test/good mark

✳ You can choose your own pair of adjectives and theme if you wish.

✳ For each of your two adjectives note down six to eight synonyms. Use a thesaurus if it helps.

✳ Next, put each of your adjectives into an order – in which they go from least to most – so they become, for example – more hot, more slow, more small, more quiet.

✳ Don't write them out again, just give them a number to show the order.

✳ Finally write your two verses. Begin verse 1 as William did with, for example, 'The day is,' and add the adjectives in your chosen order; begin verse 2 with, for example, 'But the drink is' and add the adjectives in your chosen order.

✳ Look back at William's piece and use any of his layout ideas in your own work.

 Cracking Creative Writing by David Horner © Brilliant Publications Limited. This page may be copied by the purchasing institution only.

Talking Synonyms

I'm talking funny,
I'm talking ridiculous,
I'm talking amusing, jokey, comical.
I'm talking funny-ha-ha, humorous, laugh-out-loud,
I'm talking custard pie.
I'm talking funny.

Extract from group piece

Synonyms are words that mean the same, or nearly the same.

And now it's your turn. Read all the details below before you start writing.

✻ Here are some adjectives that have several synonyms:

small   hot   clever   good   silly   noisy   sad   big

✻ Choose any one of those words and, first of all, write as long a list of synonyms for your chosen word as you can think of.

✻ Now write your synonym piece in the style of the group example above. Start each line, 'I'm talking', and then follow it with one, two or three of your found synonyms.

✻ Make the last line of your piece a repeat of the opening line. This will remind people of the original word.

✻ **Hint 1:** You are making a mini-thesaurus. If you get stuck for synonyms for your word, look in a published thesaurus for ones you might have missed. Add them to your collection.

✻ **Hint 2:** When you have finished a synonym piece, why not try an antonym piece to go with it? Antonyms are words with opposite meanings. So, for example, hot/cold, laugh/cry.

✻ **Hint 3**: Now here are some verbs that have lots of synonyms. Make a synonym piece for any one of them.

speak   move   laugh   eat   look   take   cook   get

✻ **Hint 4:** These pieces can make very useful table or wall display items. Or, get together with friends and perform a number of them – to show off the riches of the English language!

A War of Words

A War of Words
It was so exciting, that William Shakespeare wanted to turn it into a play.
> No, it was so boring, that even the chairs we sat on fell fast asleep.

It was so noisy, that the fish in the sea covered their ears.
> No, it was so quiet, that I could hear a man breathing in a library in another country.

It was so delicious, that I cried when there was no more.
> No, it was so disgusting, that everyone shouted for school dinners instead.
> > *Isaac and Raoul*

Now it's your turn.

First, read all the details below before you start your writing.

✳ This exercise is all about opposites. Pairs of words – adjectives – that have opposite meanings. For example, hot and cold; funny and sad; easy and difficult. Such words are called **antonyms**.

✳ Look back at the antonyms in Isaac and Raoul's work.

✳ Now write the title at the top of your page.

✳ Your writing will be like two people talking – well, really, arguing! You can hear the two voices disagreeing in Isaac and Raoul's work.

✳ It's important we don't know what they are arguing about! All that matters, is that they can't agree, and the way they exaggerate their ideas for dramatic effect.

✳ The pairs of lines always start in the same way:
> *It was so…*
> *No, it was so…*

✳ Next come the two opposing adjectives and finally the pairs of lines finish with a relative clause, beginning 'that…'.

✳ Begin by writing the pairs of openings; then add your antonyms + 'that'.

✳ Look at each adjective again and go on to write the wildest, most exaggerated finishing clause to back up your adjectives. Remember what the boys wrote above:
> *It was so delicious, that I cried when there was no more.*
> *No, it was so disgusting, that everyone shouted for school dinners instead.*

✳ Aim to write at least three pairs of sentences and find a friend to read the argument out loud with. You'll have to be dramatic and very over the top!

 Cracking Creative Writing by David Horner © Brilliant Publications Limited. *This page may be copied by the purchasing institution only.*

Meet the Modals

> *I can swim 50 metres now, though I can't swim up a waterfall.*
> *I could swim when I was only 4 years old, but I couldn't swim in a bowl of cold porridge.*
> *I shall swim every day on holiday, although I shall not swim in a thunder storm.*
> *I might swim to France one day, even though I might not swim back again!*
>
> Eric

And so now you've met a few modals – **modal verbs**, in fact. The modal verbs are those extra verbs immediately before the main verb – 'swim' in Eric's poem.

Here are all the main modal verbs:

>*might   should   will   must   shall   can   would   may   could*

A modal is a helping (or auxiliary) verb – it helps us change the meaning of the main verb. Look back at Eric's piece to see this very clearly.

Now it's your turn. Be sure you read all the details below before you start writing.

✳   You will need one main verb to go with the modal. Here are some to choose from:

>*run   make   live   eat   fly   buy   talk   play   learn   go   write   swap   watch*

✳   Here are the things to remember:

Use the same main verb throughout.

Write a positive and negative for each modal verb. For example: will / won't, could / couldn't, may / may not.

Join the positive and negative halves of each sentence together with a conjunction. Eric used four different conjunctions and here are three more for you to choose from:

>*however   even if   yet*

✳   Aim to use at least four of the modal verbs to go with your main verb.

✳   You could put the two halves of each sentence on separate lines, with your chosen conjunction beginning the second half.

What if Things Could Talk?

The Words of the School Window

I am one among lots. I let in light, so you can see and on hot days I will be opened to let in fresh air for you. I get looked through by everyone, although no one seems to notice that I'm here. On my outside I am always covered in rain and dust. I love it when I get cleaned so I can shine again. I'm afraid that one day I will be broken.

Aurelio

Well, what if things could talk? What would they say about themselves and their lives? Does the fridge like being so cold all the time? Does the swing in the park enjoy us sitting on it? Would the family car prefer to stay in the garage, or is it excited to come out?

Now it's your turn. Be sure you read all the details below before you start writing.

✱ Choose a thing, large or small, and imagine you are that thing.

✱ You must always remember that things never do anything for themselves. They always have things done to them. In other words, things are never active, they're only acted on – in other words things are passive.

✱ So, the passive form of verbs becomes the ideal way of creating the life of a thing.

✱ Here are some examples of the passive at work:

The photocopier has been broken.
A strange noise was heard outside.
Homework will be set.
I am being watched.

✱ You see how in those sentences we are only told what has been done. Who, or what were the doers, we don't know.

✱ Now, don't forget – you are becoming a thing. You have between six and eight sentences to bring yourself to life. In each one, describe something that happens to you each day. You don't have to use the passive form in every line – only where you think it works well.

✱ **Hint:** Don't say what your thing feels about its life. By just telling of some of your daily experiences, you leave your readers to sense those feelings for themselves.

 Cracking Creative Writing by David Horner © Brilliant Publications Limited. *This page may be copied by the purchasing institution only.*

Collective Nouns

A slithering of snakes,
A tickle of spiders,
A whiteness of clouds,
A hush of libraries,
A genie of smoke,
A dribble of strawberries,
An eternity of homeworks.

Aaron and Moira

First, read all the details below before you start your writing.

✻ You know what a noun is – a thing. A **collective noun** is the term we use for a group of things. For example, a flock of sheep, a bunch of flowers, a class of students.

✻ Here are some rarer ones you might not know: a tissue of lies, a hand of bananas, a murder of crows.

✻ All of these collective nouns – and many, many more – were invented in the past.

✻ And now it is your turn. You are going to make up some new collective nouns.

✻ How many can you invent? Write down lots to start with – quickly. Then look back through them all and choose your best ones. Keep between eight and ten.

✻ To get you started, here are six nouns:

pirates
drink cans
snails
ambulances
computer games
dentists

✻ Invent a collective noun to describe a group of any of them.

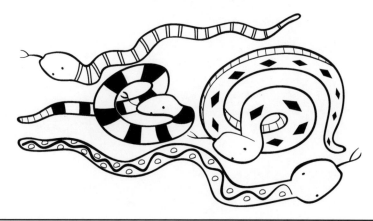

Sound Pictures

> **The Football Match**
>
> **Pheeeeep.**
>> Tip tap. **Tip tap.** Scream. Smash. **Boo.** Clatter. **Aaww.**
>> Tip tap. **Whizz.** Roar. **Tip tap.** Slam. **Clatter.** Boo. **Crunch.** Gasp.
>> **Tip tap.** Tip tap. **Thwack.** Tip tap. **Whack.** Oohh. **Aahh.** Groan. **Cheer.**
>>> **Pheeeeep.**
>>> *Dion, Anton, Zeb*

All the words in that sound picture sound like what they mean. The technical term for such words is **onomatopoeia**. You say it *on-oh-mat-oh-pea-yah*.

Now it's your turn. Read all the details below before you start writing.

✳ There are lots and lots of onomatopoeic words in English. You've known about them ever since you first sang about Old MacDonald's Farm with its mooing cows, clucking hens, etc.

✳ Here are some ideas of scenes for your sound picture, plus a few onomatopoeic words to get you started:

  • A factory and its machines: bang, honk, whirr
  • A zoo: roar, hiss, squawk
  • A superhero battle: zap, pow, wham
  • A road accident: crash, scream, nee-naw
  • A forest: snap, rustle, cuckoo

✳ Choose any one of these – or one of your own ideas, if you like. You just need a scene where you get lots of different noises.

✳ Begin by noting down all the words you can think of for your scene. A thesaurus can be a big help to you here. Look up any one word to see what others it offers.

✳ Now write your sound picture, using only your sound words in the order you like them – and feel free to repeat any of the words as often as you like if it fits the overall sound picture.

A One-sentence Wonder

> *Crouching like a big cat,*
> *gleaming in the morning sun,*
> *engine purring like ten cheetahs,*
> *then suddenly growling like a mad dog,*
> *red as a dragon's blood,*
> *ready as a penalty taker's boot,*
> *the Ferrari waits.*
>
> Dominic

First, read Dominic's poem again. How many sentences has he written? That's right, just one.

And what a good one! In that sentence, the subject, – the red Ferrari – comes last. The sentence holds the main idea until the very end. The reader is kept in suspense as the details unfold, line by line, until the subject is revealed.

There's a grammatical name for sentences made like this. They are **periodic sentences**.

And now it's your turn. Read all the details before you start.

✳ Choose a subject for your one-sentence poem. Something you like, something that means a lot to you. It could be an animal, a time of year, your bedroom, another car.

✳ To begin, note down all the important details about your chosen subject. You can do this on a piece of scrap paper if you like.

✳ Now, simply write your sequence of details, one below the other in the order you have chosen; have the actual subject of the poem – the pay-off – last.

✳ **Hint:** Put a comma after each one-line detail and don't forget the full stop to finish your periodic sentence.

A Five Line Nightmare

The pale moon is slowly hiding behind a cloud.
Tall trees are twisting their branches together over me.
The darkness seems to be wrapping me up like a cold cloak.
A tiny figure is shuffling towards me.
One bony finger is beckoning me to come closer.

Angharad

Now it's your turn.

Read all the details below before you start your writing.

✳   First, choose one of these three landscapes: an old house; a forest; a fairground.

✳   For your chosen landscape, think of five elements or details that you can imagine there and note each one down.

✳   Number the five details 1-5, with 1 being the detail furthest away from your eye on to 5, which is the one nearest to you.

✳   Look back at Angharad's poem to see what details she chose.

✳   Work through the details in order and make each detail into a sentence. Sentences need one main verb, so choose your verb carefully - think what each of your details is doing, or what is happening to it.

✳   Write each of your 5 lines with the verb in the progressive form, as in *reading, writing, thinking*. This form describes events as they are happening. Your readers will feel the nightmare as if it is happening to them - and coming closer to them with every line!

✳   Look again at Angharad's poem to see what verbs she chose and what she added to complete each atmospheric sentence.

Shape Up

If I were a circle,
I'd be a DVD, a bike wheel,
a yellow frisbee flying through the air to you.

If I were a cone,
I'd be a traffic cone, an ice cream cone,
A party hat at my own birthday party!

Flora and Ethan (extract)

Now it's your turn. Be sure you read all the details below before you start writing.

✱ We all have to learn the names of 2D and 3D shapes. Here are the most common ones:

2D: circle, square, triangle, rectangle, oval, diamond

3D: cube, cuboid, cylinder, sphere, cone, pyramid

✱ These might seem strange names at first, but fortunately, we can find all of these shapes in real world objects, as Flora and Ethan did.

✱ Begin by choosing at least one 2D and one 3D shape. Note down three objects for each of your shapes.

✱ You can set your poem out as you wish but if you want it to be like Flora and Ethan's, here are the steps:

✱ Write your poem's opening line, 'If I were a'. This slightly strange verb form is called the subjunctive. We use it to suggest a wish, a possibility, something that might happen. You can write, 'If I was a' and that would be correct too.

✱ Next, add your chosen 2D shape.

✱ Start line 2, 'I'd be a' and write two of your chosen objects.

✱ Line 3 has your last object and here add some details to bring the object more to life for your reader.

✱ Now repeat this process for your chosen 3D shape.

✱ Each verse with its three items reminds the reader of the many real-world objects that are particular geometric shapes.

✱ **Hint:** If you have time, try writing a verse for all 12 of the shapes mentioned above. Then make a book or poster of your verses to help young children learn the names of each shape. You can illustrate your writing too.

Supercalifragilisticexpialidocious

Supercalifragilisticexpialidocious

Great word, eh? And we know exactly when it was invented: 1964, for the Disney film, 'Mary Poppins'.

First of all, be sure you can say it correctly. To do this, just say each little bit of the word to yourself and then join the bits up as you get quicker and more confident. Like this: *super-cali-fragi-listic-expi-ali-doci-ous.*

In 'Mary Poppins', the word is used to mean very good, wonderful. So, we know it's an adjective. And when we look at those bits of the word again, we can see clearly that it starts with a prefix – super – and ends with a suffix – ious.

Super as a prefix means 'greater than', as in Superman: greater than a man. And we use the suffix -ious to make adjectives from nouns. So, victory becomes victorious, study becomes studious.

Here are eight more prefixes similar to super- :
ultra-, extra-, trans-, omni-, maxi-, epi-, macro-, poly-.
Here are eight more suffixes similar to -ious:
-able, -esque, -ish, -ful, -ic, -ical, -al, -ive.

Now it's your turn. You are going to invent some brand new - and very long adjectives! Like these:
extragreaterrificoolful
omnidifficultoughardable
macrotastyummyesque

✳ You need pencil, paper and, most important, a thesaurus.

✳ To get you started, here are some adjectives with lots of synonyms – words meaning the same:
good   bad   hot   cold   tasty   big   little   clever   loud

✳ Look up any one of these in your thesaurus and make a word-string, linking an adjective that ends with a certain letter to another that starts with the same letter. Just like those three examples above.

✳ Now add any of the prefixes to the start and a suffix to the end and you have your new word.

✳ Can you make a new word longer than the 34 letters of supercalifragilisticexpialidocious?

✳ Ask friends to try pronouncing your new words.

Good, Better, Best

> **Angry** is my mum if I make her late in the morning.
> **Calm** is a classroom when we are all reading.
>
> **Angrier** is a sky full of thunder and lightning.
> **Calmer** is the sea when the wind doesn't blow.
>
> **Angriest** is my dad if his team has lost.
> **Calmest** is my dog asleep under the table.
> *Isabelle and Rani*

Now it is your turn.

First, read all the details below before you start your writing.

✱ All adjectives have a basic form, a comparative form and a superlative form. For example: hot, hotter, hottest and big, bigger, biggest. A lot of adjectives also have opposites: here they'll be cold, colder, coldest and small, smaller, smallest.

✱ To begin, choose two adjectives that are opposites. Write down their basic, comparative and superlative forms as a note to yourself.

✱ Your poem will have three short verses – one verse for each form of the adjectives. These verses are:

> *First basic adjective + 'is'*
> *Second basic adjective + 'is'*
>
> *First comparative adjective + 'is'*
> *Second comparative adjective + 'is'*
>
> *First superlative adjective + 'is'*
> *Second superlative adjective + 'is'*

✱ Add some interesting details to your six lines to help a reader see just what you are imagining and describing.

The Great English Word Swap

> In Manchester did Queen Elizabeth
> a wonderful tower build:
> where Class 4, the cleverest children, climbed
> on steps terrifying to everyone
> up to a sun filled sky.
> *Extract from class-made poem*

Now it's your turn. Be sure you read all the details below before you start writing. As well as your writing materials, you need a dictionary and a book of poems.

✳ Look through the book of poems and choose a poem to work on – one short poem or part of a longer one. Read the poem through several times.

Here are the rules of the game:

✳ You are about to write a genuinely fresh piece by changing lots of the original poem's words. You can swap words as often as you like. But you must keep the grammar and punctuation of the original poem.

✳ You can swap any words in the original poem for words of your own - but you must swap a noun for a noun, a verb for a verb and so on. Don't feel you have to swap every word. Keep the little ones, or maybe swap a little word for one with an opposite meaning. So, *down* for *up*, *without* for *with*, *but* for *and*.

✳ You can make other changes. For example, make singular nouns plural; change a verb from past to present.

✳ If your chosen poem rhymes, don't struggle to keep the rhyme scheme.

✳ If you are unsure what grammatical group a word belongs to – noun, adverb, etc. – use your dictionary to check.

✳ When you are happy with everything, make a final draft and perhaps also a copy of the original poem, so your readers can see the differences.

✳ Here is the original text the class word-swapped. It is the opening to 'Kubla Khan', written in 1797 by Samuel Taylor Coleridge.

> *In Xanadu did Kubla Khan*
> *A stately pleasure-dome decree:*
> *Where Alph, the sacred river, ran*
> *Through caverns measureless to man*
> *Down to a sunless sea.*

Similes for Surrealists

> **The world is blue like an orange.**
> *Paul Eluard**

First, read all the details below before you start your writing.

* I bet you didn't expect that line ending! Try reading the first five words out loud to friends and ask them to guess the next two words. No one, I promise you, will say, an orange.

* And that, in a nutshell, is surrealism. Surrealist art never does what you expect. It doesn't like the expected, the obvious, the normal. It wants to tease you by being different. And above all, it wants to get you thinking differently.

* If the poet had wanted to write an obvious line, he'd have written, 'The world is round like an orange'. Or, 'The world is blue like an eye.'

* But he didn't. And now it is your turn. Start by writing Paul Eluard's line at the top of your page.

* Underneath, begin line 2, 'An orange is' – then add an adjective which is true about an orange. Then write *like*. Now finish the line with the oddest, weirdest, most unexpected ending to the simile you can come up with.

* So, you might say, 'An orange is juicy like a pebble'.

* Begin line 3 with the ending to line 2 and again add your truthful adjective and *like*, before completing the simile as strangely as you can.

* Don't forget that you can make your simile using 'as' instead of 'like' every time. So that second line would be:

  An orange is as juicy as a pebble

* This all helps give your writing a bit of useful variety.

* Just write as many lines as you have time for. Perhaps you can even have a last line that ends with the poem's opening phrase. So — like the world.

* Paul Eluard was French, and he lived from 1895 to 1952. In French, that line goes, 'La terre est bleue comme une orange'.

The Loaf of My Life

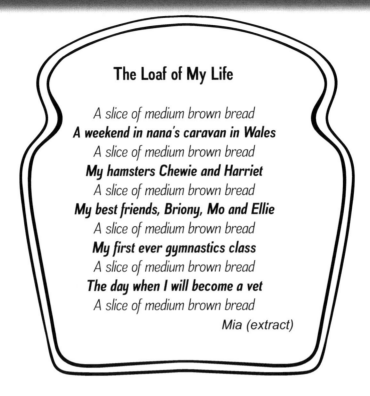

The Loaf of My Life

A slice of medium brown bread
A weekend in nana's caravan in Wales
A slice of medium brown bread
My hamsters Chewie and Harriet
A slice of medium brown bread
My best friends, Briony, Mo and Ellie
A slice of medium brown bread
My first ever gymnastics class
A slice of medium brown bread
The day when I will become a vet
A slice of medium brown bread

Mia (extract)

Now it's your turn. Be sure you read all the details below before you start writing.

✳ You are going to make a giant written sandwich.

✳ Let's start with the bread. Decide on the thickness of your slices: thin or medium or thick?

✳ Next, choose the kind of bread you'd like from this list:

wholewheat   white   multigrain   sourdough   rye   brown

✳ Now write down your first slice of your chosen bread. For example, A slice of thin whole-wheat bread. You will repeat this bread line on every other line of your piece, obviously.

✳ Now the fillings. These fillings won't be the usual food stuff. This sandwich will hold all your favourite things – past, present and future – as in Mia's piece.

✳ A sliced loaf has between 14 and 22 slices if we ignore the end-pieces. So, you need a minimum of 13 and a maximum of 21 fillings.

✳ Each filling will be one of your favourite things, people, places, animals, experiences. Be sure to include ideas from your very early years all the way into your hopes and plans for your future. Again, look back at that extract from Mia's loaf for examples of this.

✳ Don't worry about any long lines – sandwiches always have some bits sticking out!

✳ When you have rough-drafted your loaf, draw the outline of a typical bread slice on a fresh piece of paper and write your final draft inside it.

 Cracking Creative Writing by David Horner © Brilliant Publications Limited. *This page may be copied by the purchasing institution only.*

Meet Some Colourful Characters

> Robert Red, Robert Red,
>   balanced a broomstick on his head.
> Bella Blue, Bella Blue,
>   thinks that 3 plus 9 is 2.
> Yasmin Yellow, Yasmin Yellow,
>   plays the saxophone and cello.
> Gregory Grey, Gregory Grey,
>   won the lottery – and gave it away.
>
> *Callum (extract)*

Some colours, for example, black, white, brown, green and grey, are also common surnames. However, other colours – pink, purple, scarlet, cream, peach and lots more – aren't used in this way. Have you ever met someone with the surname Beige? Or Aquamarine? Thought not.

Now it's your turn. Be sure you read all the details below before you start writing.

✳ Note down eight to ten colours. You can start with the ones Callum used in his poem, if you like. Think of the rest for yourself.

✳ Pick any one of your chosen colours. This word is now a surname, so it needs a capital letter. It also needs a first name. This can be a boy's or a girl's name – but make it alliterative, so the two names begin with the same letter. So, Robert Red, Bella Blue.

✳ Make the first line of your poem by writing the name twice. This lets you make the second, rhyming line longer – and, hopefully funnier!

✳ Now write the second rhyming line. A good tip is to think of words that rhyme with the colour, then choose the one you like best and compose a line to fit it.

✳ Write as many pairs of lines – each one is called a rhyming couplet – as you have time for.

✳ **Hint**: Comic poems like these work best if the two lines have roughly the same pattern when read aloud. The two lines seem to belong together, as here:

Yasmin Yellow, Yasmin Yellow,
plays the saxophone and cello.

The Furniture Game

This person is a comfortable armchair.
She's a heatwave at the seaside
She's spaghetti bolognese with garlic bread.
She's Matilda Wormwood.
My best friend is all the rings around Saturn.

Madeleine

This is an old writing game and now it's your turn to play.

First, read all the details below before you start your writing.

Now, choose somebody to write about that you know well.

✳ You are going to change this person into some different things.

✳ To begin, write, 'This person is' and then ask yourself: if this person was a piece of furniture, what would it be? Write your answer down to finish line 1.

✳ You can now write as many lines as you've time for by asking yourself lots more 'If this person was…' questions. For example, what kind of weather, what food, what living thing in the sea, what piece of clothing, what plant?

✳ The answers you get to your questions give you the words and lines to bring your chosen person to life.

✳ Each line is a metaphor – you are seeing a person as something else; something that suits them but is completely different.

Cracking Creative Writing by David Horner © Brilliant Publications Limited. This page may be copied by the purchasing institution only.

What Is the New Moon?

What Is the New Moon?

The New Moon is a banana.
    big enough to feed the world.
The New Moon is a pirate ship
    sailing on black water.
The New Moon is a dog's tail
    wagging to us from far away.
The New Moon is a boomerang.
    It flies away and always comes back to us.

Nathan

First, read all the details below before you start your writing.

✱ This is an exercise to help you create some great metaphors.

✱ Metaphors say one thing is another thing.

✱ We use metaphors to make what we say and what we write more colourful, more vivid. If someone tells you you're a star, they don't mean you're a twinkly thing in outer space. But the metaphor does make you feel very special. It never really rains cats and dogs, but the metaphor does make that rain feel very heavy.

✱ To begin, quickly write down all the things you can think of that are the same crescent shape as the New Moon. You've just read Nathan's ideas. You might imagine a smile, a hammock, the letter C.

✱ You only need four to six things. When you have these, write the title, 'What is the New Moon?'

✱ Below the title, write 'The New Moon is' and then finish the line with any one of the things you've noted down.

✱ To make your metaphor, now write a second line below the first. This line develops the metaphor by say something interesting about the thing you've chosen.

✱ Now do the same with all the other things in your list.

✱ **Hint:** Keep the thing you like best of all until last, so your writing ends strongly!

✱ You could use this idea to write a poem called 'What is the Sun?' Think of other round things such as a plate, a drum, a clock face, etc. Then write interesting metaphors to go with them.

A Perfect Square

Each line here has eight syllables.
I was born in the eighth month, so
eight is now my lucky number.
I'm not eight now, but I once was.
8 looks like a little snowman.
I get up before eight. Sometimes.
Steven Gerrard wears number 8.
There are eight lines here. You can check.

Kate

Now it's your turn. Be sure you read all the details below before you start writing.

✳ For her Perfect Square poem, Kate chose the number 8. Obviously! But you can try the idea for any number between 5 and 11.

✳ Whatever the number you choose, the rules are these:

You must write exactly that number of lines.
There must be that number of syllables in each line.
That number must appear in every line.

✳ A reminder about syllables: a syllable is one sound in a word. So, John (1), Jonny (2), Jonathan (3). Just count the beats in a word and you'll get the number of syllables.

✳ **Hint:** When you have an idea for a line for your Perfect Square, try saying it in all sorts of different ways, to help you get a line with the right syllable count.

 Cracking Creative Writing by David Horner © Brilliant Publications Limited. This page may be copied by the purchasing institution only.

How to Write a Syllangle

> *Look,*
> *there is*
> *a monster,*
> *with scaly skin*
> *and very sharp teeth.*
> *It has started to move.*
>
> Maria and Vince (extract)

A **syllangle** is a portmanteau word. This means it is a new word made from two old ones – like romcom (from romance and comedy) and motel (from motor and hotel). Syllangle is made from the words syllable and triangle.

Syllables first. A syllable is one sound in a word. So, Caz (1), Carol (2), Caroline (3). Just count the beats in a word and you'll get the number of syllables.

Now it's your turn. There are two activities here. You can do one or both of them. Be sure you read all the details below before you start writing.

✳ **Activity 1:** First, choose one of these subjects:

> *foods   vehicles   place names   football teams   animals   films*

✳ Now you need to write down items that fit your subject – with each item just one syllable longer than the last. So, for example, if you chose animals, your first three items might be, fox, tiger, polar bear. Write the items one under the other to create a triangular shape – and your syllangle is taking shape. The challenge is to see how many items you can think of or find.

✳ **Activity 2:** That first activity used just single words or phrases. Now, what about writing a short syllangle poem, again growing by one syllable every line? First, look back at how Maria and Vince began their syllangle.

✳ Here are two more syllangle beginnings:

> *Once*
> *when I*
> *was younger*
>
> *There's*
> *a dark,*
> *dismal place*
> *beneath the bed*

✳ Use one of them – or start your own. How big will your syllangle become?

Comical Couplets

As I was walking into town,
I met a king who wore no crown.

As I was sailing in my boat,
I reached a place where sunk ships float.

As I was strolling round the zoo,
I saw a bear whose tail was blue.

As I was making up this song,
I sang some words which were all wrong.
Ivan and Liam

Those four comic rhymes were inspired by another very well-known one written by the American, William Hughes Mearns in 1922:

As I was going up the stair,
I met a man who wasn't there.

Now it's your turn. Be sure you read all the details below before you start writing.

✳ Look back at Hughes Mearns' original pair of lines – they're called a **rhyming couplet** – and you'll see the word 'who'. See where Ivan and Liam use it too.

✳ There are some other small words that begin 'wh-'. Here they are:

which   where   when   whose   while

✳ These small words are useful because they all join a main clause ('I saw a man') to a relative clause ('who wasn't there'). So, can you now use any or all of those 'wh-' words to make up more rhymes in the same style?

✳ Begin line 1 of each couplet, 'As I was' plus a verb in its progressive form (ending '-ing'). Begin the second line, 'I' plus a verb in its past tense.

✳ **Hint 1**: You might find it easier to get your rhyming words first and then build your comical couplet around them. Be as inventive as you can with the ending of your second line.

✳ **Hint 2**: As well as the rhyme, your pairs of lines need that even, regular rhythm. This comes from their alternating of unstressed and stressed syllables. As here, for example:

*As I was **strolling round** the **zoo**,*
*I **saw** a **bear** whose **tail** was **blue**.*

✳ Just say your lines to yourself over and over until you're happy with what you hear.

A Circle of Similes

The trees are as tall as the path is narrow.
The path is as dusty as our footsteps are loud.
Our footsteps are as excited as the leaves are green.
The leaves are as soft as the branches are twisted.
The branches are as bony as that beetle is black.
That beetle is as nippy as the fox is silent.
The fox is as hidden as the sunshine is warm.
The sunshine is as glittering as the trees are never-ending.

Jodie

You can see why this poem is a circle – it ends where it began. And it is full of the words 'as…as,' so there are lots of similes. This all makes it a Circle of Similes!

Now it's your turn. Be sure you read all the details below before you start writing.

✱   Choose a scene for your similes circle. It can be a scene you know well, an imaginary scene, or wherever you are writing now. For example, a fairground, the seaside, a city centre, one of the planets, a room in your house, a scene from the past.

✱   When you have chosen your scene, note down all the things you can see or imagine there. Write quickly and include everything you think of. Don't edit at this stage.

✱   Now, from your notes, choose any or all of your items and begin your similes circle.

✱   Look back at Jodie's poem and see how each item ends one line and starts the next. So, you will need two adjectives for each item.

✱   Your piece will be richer if your two adjectives suggest different features of the item.

✱   You can start where you like, but remember, to complete the circle you must end with your opening item.

Rhyme Time

> One, two, buckle my shoe.
> Three, four, knock at the door.
> Five, six, pick up sticks.
> Seven, eight, lay them straight.
> Nine, ten, a big fat hen.
>
> Eleven, twelve, dig and delve.
> Thirteen, fourteen, maids a-courting.
> Fifteen, sixteen, maids in the kitchen.
> Seventeen, eighteen, maids in waiting.
> Nineteen, twenty, my plate's empty.
>
> *Anonymous*

Now it's your turn.

First, read all the details below before you start your writing.

✳ That is an old rhyme – and you can see how we know. We don't have buckles on our shoes any more, and we don't have all those maids in our homes either!

✳ Your challenge, therefore, is to bring the rhyme up to date.

✳ Begin each line by writing its two numbers just as they are in the original. Then come up with a fresh finish to each line – which must rhyme with the second number.

✳ Aim not to use any of the rhyme words that are in the original rhyme.

✳ However, don't worry too much about getting perfect rhymes. Close ones will do, as you can see in the original rhyme's second verse.

✳ Apart from the rhymes, make the details in each line as interesting as you can. You want a reader to enjoy your new version.

✳ If you are short of time, you can just work on verse one. Or, you might get a friend to share the task with you and each of you do a verse.

Writing Rhymes for Younger Children

Doctor Foster went to Gloucester.
Doctor McGrath went to Bath.
Doctor Harris went to Paris.
But Doctor Ball went nowhere at all.

Little Miss Donnet wears a big bonnet.
Little Mrs Hughes wears teeny weeny shoes.
Little Mr Cox wears brightly coloured socks.
Little Master Dan wears a giant frying pan.

Extracts from class-made rhymes

Now it's your turn. Be sure you read all the details below before you start writing.

✳ You need a good book of nursery rhymes to research.

✳ Nursery rhymes almost always start with a good strong rhyme. Young children know this and you can use this knowledge to make new rhymes for them, simply by taking an opening line from an existing rhyme and writing more like it.

✳ You've already read the two examples above and here are some more suggestions. In each case, the key rhyme words you'll need to change are highlighted.

*Hickory dickory **dock**, the mouse ran up the **clock***
*Jack and **Jill** went up the **hill***
*Little Bo **Peep** has lost her **sheep***
*Little Tommy **Tucker** sings for his **supper***
*Hey diddle **diddle**, the cat and the **fiddle***
*Jack **Spratt** could eat no **fat***
*Three little **kittens**, they lost their **mittens***

✳ Choose one or more of these openings – or one you've found yourself in your research.

✳ Write your chosen line at the top of your page and begin composing your new lines, keeping the pattern of the original line and changing the key rhyme. You can also change other words where you feel this would work well.

✳ **Hint:** Put your best new line as your last rhyme so you end with something a bit special.

✳ When you finish one or more new rhyme collections, make a book of them, complete with colourful illustrations. Take it to a group of younger children to share it and read it with them.

Nursery Rhymes for Grown-Ups

Silence, minute child on the highest branch.

When the air-flow makes a draught, the infant's bed is going to wobble from side to side. When the main branch separates, the infant's bed is going to get lower and lower very quickly.

Vertically will descend minute child, infant's bed and absolutely everything.

Class-made poem

* Did you recognise the nursery rhyme buried under all that language? That's right: Hush-a-bye, baby, on the tree top.

* Well, the original was okay for very young children, but grown-ups need something a bit more, well, grown up.

* Grown-ups like complicated sentences and long words. And now it's your turn to write like a grown-up.

You need a book of nursery rhymes, a dictionary and a thesaurus – and read all the details below before you start writing.

* Find your nursery rhyme. Here are some for you to consider:
    Little Jack Horner
    Humpty Dumpty
    I do not like thee, Doctor Fell
    Twinkle, twinkle, little star.

* Choose from these or one you have found yourself.

* To write your grown-up version, work carefully through the original. Focus on the important words and leave the unimportant ones alone. Look back at line 1 at the top. What has not been changed? That's right, *on the*.

* You are all the time looking for synonyms, so use your thesaurus to find them. A word you have never used before is probably a good pick!

* Also, look up words in your dictionary, and sometimes use the dictionary's definition of a word, as a synonym for the word in the original rhyme.

* Oh, and no need to worry about rhyme. Most poems for grown-ups don't.

* When you have finished you will undoubtedly have increased your own word power and you're ready to impress those grown-ups!

Full Colour Haiku

> *Full moon at midnight.*
> *Earth sleeps under a blanket.*
> *The snowman stands guard.*
>
> Two chopped bananas
> in a big bowl of custard
> on a sun-bright cloth.
>
> *Blackpool supporters*
> *just for luck eat tangerines*
> *and drink Irn Bru.*
> *Oliver*

Haiku are tiny poems with tight rules: They are always three lines long; the first line must have 5 syllables; the second line must have 7 syllables; and the third line must have 5 syllables. The whole haiku – a Japanese form originally – must present a reader with a clear, vivid picture or scene.

Oh, and here's one extra rule: in your full colour haiku, you must not use the actual colour word. Oliver didn't and yet you can easily 'see' his three colour scenes.

Now it's your turn.

Read all the details below before you start writing.

✳ Begin by choosing a colour and make a list of things you can think of that are that colour.

✳ Look at your list and choose the three things you want to include in your haiku. Choose three things that will go together to make your word picture.

✳ Decide in what order you will write about your three things – and don't forget the 5, 7, 5 syllables rule.

✳ Just try drafting your idea for a line in different ways to get the syllable count right. You can say your ideas to yourself and count the syllables on your fingers – it's much quicker than writing everything down!

How Pleasant to Know Mr. Lear!

> *There was an Old Person of Leeds*
> who ate a whole packet of cornflakes.
> *She caught a fast train*
> and she travelled first class
> *until she arrived in Brazil.*
>
> Simon

That limerick begins with an opening line by Edward Lear, and then Simon decides to break the rules and go his own way.

Actually, Simon only breaks one of the rules of limerick writing: he uses no rhyme. But there are 5 lines – 2 long, then 2 short, then 1 long. And he's kept the rhythm of the limerick – each of the long lines has the usual 3 beats and the short lines each have 2 beats.

Now it's your turn. Read all the details below before you start writing. And first, read Simon's unrhymed limerick a few times, exaggerating those beats, to get the rhythm fixed for yourself.

✳ Here is how Edward Lear's limerick continues:

> *There was an Old Person of Leeds,*
> *Whose head was infected with beads;*
> *She sat on a stool*
> *And ate gooseberry fool,*
> *Which agreed with the Person of Leeds.*

✳ Here are some more of Lear's first lines:

> *There was an Old Man with a beard…*
> *There was an Old Man in a tree…*
> *There was a Young Lady of Portugal…*
> *There was an Old Man who said, 'Hush!'…*

✳ Choose one of these and write it down.

✳ Now write your four lines to complete your own unrhymed limerick. Remember to keep the limerick rhythm – and definitely no rhyming!

✳ Finally, to inspire you, here is a famous unrhymed limerick by W S Gilbert:

> *There was an old man of St Bees,*
> *Who was stung on the arm by a wasp.*
> *When asked, 'Does it hurt?'*
> *He replied, 'No, it doesn't,*
> *I'm so glad it wasn't a hornet.'*

An Acrostic Autobiography

Sam is really
A
Martian,

But he travels to earth in his
UFO
To visit London where he
Loves
Eating
Rugby balls.
                    Sam

That's what an acrostic poem does: the first letters of each line spell out a word, phrase or sentence. Even a secret message!

Now it's your turn.

First, read all the details below before you start your writing. And have a dictionary with you.

✱ Write your name down the left side of your page in capital letters. This can be your first name only, or your full name. It's up to you.

✱ Begin line 1 with your first name and then start writing your acrostic. You can have as many words as you like on each line – so long as every line starts with the correct letter.

✱ You can write a truthful acrostic autobiography about yourself, or, like Sam, you can invent a totally new, fantastical you!

✱ **Hint:** If you are stuck for words, open your dictionary at the key letter and go word hunting.

Let Us Now Praise...Very Ordinary Things

An Ode to a Pencil Sharpener!

O pencil sharpener!
> *Small silver cuboid with your one tiny blade.*
You hide down safe in my pencil case until,
when I need you, you are ready
> *to sharpen every one of my pencils and crayons.*
You never run out of ink like my pen.
You never slip like my ruler.
I hold you in my left hand and you always work. Always.
> *Glory be to you, O pencil sharpener!*

Gregory

You can clearly hear a spoken voice behind that writing. It feels at once dramatic. It's an **ode**. An ode is a poem written to a particular person or thing. That's why the word 'you' appears so often. The over-the-top style makes the poem's ordinary subject – a pencil sharpener – seem at once grand and important.

See how Gregory begins, 'O.' Words like this are called **interjections**. They at once show strong emotion. There are lots of modern ones like, Wow! Hurray! and Ouch!

Gregory ends with another traditional interjection, 'Glory be to you'. Here are some more:

Respect to you   *All hail*   *Honour to you*   *Praise to you*   *Thanks be to you*   *Bravo*

Now it's your turn. Be sure you read all the details below before you start writing.

✳ Choose an ordinary, everyday object for your ode. For example, a kettle, a rubber band, a carrier bag, a road sign.

✳ To begin, note down everything you can think of connected with your object – its shape, its colours, its purpose, where it is found, how life would be if it didn't exist.

✳ Write the title, *An Ode to* and then your chosen object.

✳ Start line 1 of the ode with any of those traditional interjections – followed by your object.

✳ Now write your lines of praise, with a fresh detail on every line. Remember, you are writing to your chosen object in a style that will make it become very, very special.

✳ Finish the ode with a different interjection from the examples above and name the object one last time.

 Cracking Creative Writing by David Horner © Brilliant Publications Limited. *This page may be copied by the purchasing institution only.*

A Bundle of Blessings

A Bundle of Blessings

Blessed be my mum and dad.
Blessed be the Premier League.
A blessing on my brother Louis.
A blessing on the total untidiness of my bedroom.
Blessed be my green Ridgeback bike.
Blessed be my Nike boots.
Blessed be spaghetti bolognese and garlic bread.
Blessings on my nanas and grandad.
Blessed be Minecraft.
A blessing on grown-ups and their grumpiness.

Niall

A blessing is a wish for the happiness and well-being of someone or something.

In the Bible, in Matthew's Gospel, Jesus speaks to his disciples in the famous Sermon on the Mount. In this sermon Jesus includes eight blessings. These are usually called the Eight Beatitudes. Among the eight, Jesus offers blessings on the meek, the merciful, the pure in heart and the peacemakers.

And today we still offer blessings. Surely nobody sneezes without someone saying, 'Bless you!'

Now it's your turn to offer some more blessings. Be sure you read all the details below before you start writing.

✱ You can bless people you know, your heroes, any particular group of people; also, animals, objects, places; the qualities in people you like and want to wish well. Nothing is too trivial for you to include if that thing is important to you. Be generous!

✱ Write the title, A Bundle of Blessings at the head of your paper.

✱ Begin each blessing with the phrase, 'A blessing on', 'Blessed be' or 'Blessings on'.

✱ Write quickly. You can write as many blessings as you have time for, in any order they come into your mind.

Permissions and References

Russian Dolls, page 10
The inspiration for this activity is a line, 'I placed a jar in Tennessee' from the poem 'Anecdote of the Jar' by Wallace Stevens. The full poem can be found at: https://www.poetryfoundation.org/poetrymagazine/poems/14575/anecdote-of-the-jar

Spot the Difference, page 15
The idea for this activity comes from a poem by John Hegley called, 'The Differences between Dogs and Deckchairs'. It can be found in *New & Selected Potatoes*, by John Hegley, published by Bloodaxe in 2013.

No, No, No, November, page 19
The full version of Thomas Hood's poem, 'No!' (sometimes referred to as 'November'), can be found at: https://poets.org/poem/no

It's a Crazy, Mixed up World…, page 20
The idea for this activity comes from Charles Causley's poem from *'Quack!' said the Billy-Goat*, by Charles Causley and Barbara Firth, published by Candlewick Press in 1999.

The Most Mysterious Martian Alphabet, page 26
The John Lennon poem, 'A is for Parrot' can be found in *The Orchard Book of Poems*, edited by Adrian Mitchell and published by Orchard books in 1996.

A Day in the Life of…, page 37
The inspiration for this activity is 'Composed upon Westminster Bridge, September 3, 1802' by William Wordsworth. It can be found at: https://www.poetryfoundation.org/poems/45514/composed-upon-westminster-bridge-september-3-1802

Tonight at Noon, page 38
'Tonight at Noon' from *The Mersey Sound*, by Adrian Henri, Published by Penguin Classics, 2007. Copyright © Adrian Henri. Reproduced by permission of the Estate c/o Rogers, Coleridge & White Ltd., 20 Powis Mews, London W11 1JN

Incredible Ice Creams, page 45
The extracts 'TUTTI-FRUTTI STEWED TOMATO', 'AVOCADO BRUSSELS SPROUT' and 'CAULIFLOWER COLA MUSTARD' come from Jack Prelutsky's poem, 'Bleezer's Ice Cream'. The full poem can be found at: https://poets.org/poem/bleezers-ice-cream

Riddle-y-Diculous!, page 52
The idea for this activity comes from a poem by Martyn Wiley and Ian McMillan called 'Three Riddled Riddles'. It can be found in *This Poem Doesn't Rhyme*, edited by Gerard Benson and published by Puffin Books in 1992.

I'd Rather…, page 58
The line 'I'd rather be a hammer than a nail' comes from the song, 'El Cóndor Pasa' (If I Could) by singer/songwriter Paul Simon.

Fourteen Questions to an Alien, page 62
The inspiration for this activity is 'The Tyger' by William Blake. It can be found at: https://www.poetryfoundation.org/poems/43687/the-tyger

Impossible Demands, page 66
The example child's poem on this page uses the title of a poem by Emily Dickinson, 'Bring Me The Sunset In A Cup'. This poem can be found in full at: https://www.poemhunter.com/poem/bring-me-the-sunset-in-a-cup/

Weather Warnings, page 74
The extract 'Don't take off…' comes from Kenneth Koch's poem, 'The Aesthetics of Being in Haiti' from *The Collected Poems of Kenneth Koch* by Kenneth Koch, copyright © 2005 by The Kenneth Koch Literary Estate. Used by permission of Alfred A. Knopf, an imprint of the Knopf Doubleday Publishing Group, a division of Penguin Random House LLC. All rights reserved.

Thirteen Things, page 75
The inspiration for this activity is the poem, 'Thirteen Ways of Looking at a Blackbird' written by Wallace Stephens. It can be found at: https://www.poetryfoundation.org/poems/45236/thirteen-ways-of-looking-at-a-blackbird

Also referred to is 'Fourteen Ways of Touching the Peter' by George MacBeth, which appears in *Collected Poems 1958-1982* by George MacBeth © George MacBeth 1989.

The Great English Word Swap, page 94
The poem 'Kubla Khan' by Samuel Taylor Coleridge can be found at: https://www.poetryfoundation.org/poems/43991/kubla-khan

Similes for Surrealists, page 95
'La terre est bleue comme une orange' ('The world is blue like an orange') is from Paul Eluard's book of poems, *L'amour la poésie,* originally published in 1929, republished by Black Widow Press in 2007. The French poem can be found at: http://eluardexplique.free.fr/amour/laterreestbleue.html

Comical Couplets, page 102
The inspiration for this activity is the extract 'As I was going up the stair…' from the poem 'Antigonish' by William Hughes Mearns. The full poem can be found at: https://en.wikipedia.org/wiki/Antigonish_(poem)